SO-BFC-889

Man of the House

Man of the House

Reflections on Life with Dogs,
Divas, and a Bunch of Little Dudes
Who Keep Calling Me Dad

Chris Erskine

RODALE

Book design by Christopher Rhoads

Library of Congress Cataloging-in-Publication Data

Erskine, Chris.
   Man of the house : reflections on life with dogs, divas, and a bunch of little dudes who keep
   calling me dad / by Chris Erskine.
      p.   cm.
   ISBN-13 978-1-59486-391-2   hardcover
   ISBN-10 1-59486-391-1   hardcover
   1. Fatherhood—Humor.   2. Father and child—Humor.   I. Title.
   PN6231.F37E77   2006
   814'.6—dc22   2006002359

Distributed to the trade by Holtzbrinck Publishers

2   4   6   8   10   9   7   5   3   1   hardcover

We inspire and enable people to improve their lives and the world around them
For more of our products visit **rodalestore.com** or call 800-848-4735

To all the little people . . .

Contents

FOREWORD

This books springs from a mind clogged with seven different computer passwords, a dozen PIN numbers, assorted sports stats, three tasteless jokes, and the Lord's Prayer. If it makes any sense at all, it is due to the patience and talents of my literary agent B.J. Robbins, editor Zachary Schisgal, and the other skilled folks at Rodale.

This is mostly new work, some 30 fresh essays all dealing with the tiny joys and random pratfalls of contemporary fatherhood. I'm also proud to include a dozen or so past columns from the *Los Angeles Times*.

Someone once said that we talk least about the things we think about the most. Here, I talk about it all—the heartaches, the rewards, the longings, the lust. I hope these paternal ramblings are good for a few laughs. If you like them, please give my family credit for sharing their lives. If you don't, it's only because I failed to do them justice. For I have never won the lottery, or even the gift basket at the school fair. But with them, I hit the jackpot every single day. A lucky man, I.

—*Chris Erskine*

1

Mothers, Goosed

WE ARE NOT so different from you. Four kids. Three bedrooms. Two mortgages. Our little town is affluent, though we are not. Most of our waking hours are devoted to our children, handsome kids with manes of mink.

Our woodwork is nicked, as are we. The dents and dings of early parenthood run up and down our burled knees. Are we happy? You decide.

When we load the minivan for the trip to school, the night's condensation streaks the window like tears. The seats are cool, even in summer. The kids lift their backpacks aboard as if crushing sandbags onto an earthen dike. Umph. Clunk. Scratch. Did I mention the car's a little past its prime? Picture Patton's jeep.

And off we go across the boulevard, the relentless and invisible people of suburban America. My youngest daughter is in the seat next to me, contemplating her teeth. The neighbor girl, Elizabeth, sits still as cinderblock in the backseat, fearing I may actually speak to her. Speaking with an adult is a common adolescent concern.

As we pass the gas station, I wave to Charlie, my Lebanese mechanic, not to mention a devout-demented Packer fan. Near the garden shop, I see Susan, the dentist's lovely wife. She smiles, and I am reminded of the importance of quality dental care.

In the minivan, meanwhile, there is all the cheer of a postal truck. No one speaks except me. Every attempt to engage them in conversation is met with mere shrugs, grunts, and various bodily noises.

"Nice day," I say.

Shrug.

"The new king must be a golfer," I try.

Grunt.

I've found, after 10 years of carpools, that I can pretty much throw out any sort of nonsensical remark, and they will nod, shrug, grunt, or fart a response. From what I can tell, they are saving the best of themselves for their friends. For Marisa or Kate. Abby or Amanda. Why waste precious wit on your old man? We'll be at school soon enough.

"Do you think," I ask, "that condensation is water? Or is it some sort of mystic force?"

Nod.

"Because it seems to me to be like witchcraft," I say. "It happens mostly at night."

Burp.

These are the conversations we have on the way to school. It reminds me that even if you have children this can be a very lonely country.

Yet, I refuse to give in. Take it as a challenge, I tell myself. You can either sit back and say, "Hey, they're just kids. Let them sulk," or you can try to stimulate them with gags and nonsequiturs.

"I love a good pickle," I say. "You?"

"Sure, Dad," the little girl says.

See? You can get through to them. You can break into their little "Me-Worlds" of selfishness and fear. They worry most about being embarrassed in front of their friends, of sitting alone at lunch, of wearing (oh-my-god!) the wrong shoes. These are all legitimate concerns, especially when you're 12 or 13. I am not belittling them. I am here only to try to understand and help.

By engaging them in silly talk, I try to reduce their level of early morning anxiety. Over the course of 20 years, in two states, three school systems, and 12 grade levels, it has worked hardly at all.

"Did I mention," I ask, "that I'm having lunch with the Dalai Lama?"

Shrug.

"We're meeting at Hooters," I say.

Nod.

"He's crazy for their wings," I say.

Nothing.

"Hey, does this mole look funny to you?" I ask.

My request for free medical advice is met with indifference. This mole could kill me one day. Moles are just places for bad news to land. Little heliports of hell.

"Oh, I guess it's just some Magic Marker," I say as we pull up to the drop-off point.

Obviously relieved, they get out of the car and tug madly at their backpacks, which hit the pavement like a 12-pound sledge.

"Bye, Dad," my daughter burps.

"Thanks, Mr. Erskine," says her little friend.

See? You can get through. And boy is it worth it.

Back home, the mood is not quite so warm or welcoming. The dog needs to go out. To hear my wife tell it, his bladder could at any moment explode.

"Will you walk him?" she asks.

"Did I tell you about the Dalai Lama?" I ask.

"Just walk him," she says.

More and more, I am a morning person. I rise with that first siren of dawn, fix a little breakfast, and lust after the TV weather girl. Each morning, the routine is the same. I drive them to school, walk the dog, and go for a little run. I do it cheerfully and without any apparent compensation.

"Come on," I say to the dog.

"Sure," the toddler says.

The toddler thinks everything I say to the dog is really directed to him. When I ask the dog to go out, the toddler wraps his sticky toddler arms around my neck.

"Let's go," the toddler says.

"Who washes you?" I ask him.

"You do," he says.

"That's no excuse," I say.

He is like a human resin bag—sticky and about 2 pounds in weight, most of it shoes. If I have a lot of lifting to do, or a baseball to throw, I will first run my hands along his arms and ankles, building up resin for the task at hand. It makes lifting slippery objects so much easier.

"Come on," he says.

"Where we going?"

"We're walking the dog," he says and tugs on my furry, sunburned neck.

And the three of us go down the quiet street: me, the toddler, and the little dog. Every once in a while, the toddler will dismount to sniff a dandelion or lick a Styrofoam cup he finds in the gardenias. To him, it's all nature.

"Don't touch that," I'll say when he eyes another piece of litter.

"Why not?"

"Germs," I'll say.

He claims to like germs, and anything else nature tosses his way. Recently, in the backyard, he handed me a live bumble bee. He's always handing me things he finds outside: flowers, seed pods, beer caps. So when he showed me the bee, I didn't think much of it. Till it moved.

"Arrrrghh" I said.

"What?"

"That's a bee!"

"So?"

I think the toddler was trying to squeeze honey from its tiny bumble-bee rump. Or maybe he was just playing with it, the way he plays with kittens. In any case, I knocked it quickly from his sticky little hand, then stepped on it, which the toddler enjoyed immensely. He may be a naturalist, but he is no fool. He spent the next 5 minutes killing ants he spotted on the flagstone path.

"What's he doing?" his mother called out from the back porch as the toddler chicken-danced around the backyard.

"Making the world a safer place," I said.

"Okay," she said, satisfied.

This particular morning, he hasn't killed anything yet. He stops to sniff each dandelion, touching it with his nose as if pollinating it. He crushes some lavender in his fist, then smiles. He throws a rock.

The dog, meanwhile, runs his belly through the juniper plants, which freshens his undercarriage with a minty scent. As the weather warms, I am always walking him through the juniper plants. Nature's dog wash.

"Come on, boys," I finally say, tugging them both toward home. "I'll fix you some flan."

∾

I jog along my usual morning route, smelling the chorizo cooking at the Mexican takeout place. Except for this, our little suburb is suspiciously without breakfast scents. The animal lust that bacon brings is an increasingly rare thing. Eventually, I guess, we will all live forever.

Past the workout salons and dry cleaners I go. Past the gas station, throbbing with activity, and the real estate offices that dot every block.

I pad lightly past the pizza place and breathe deep as I round the donut shop. I stop to let the garbage truck clear a driveway. Lawn sprinklers lick my shoes.

They shave the sidewalks here. You heard me correctly, they shave the sidewalks. At the seams, where one slab of concrete is higher than the next, some machine has planed down the concrete so that the two seams are even. If suburbs aren't all about perfection, then why are they shaving the sidewalks?

I turn and enter the neighborhoods. Talk about perfection. As I pass the mansions of suburban L.A., I realize that you can pretty much figure out a home's floor plan by the placement of the chimney. Find the chimney stack, and you've located a family room. Right next to that, a kitchen.

There are some houses that catch my eye every day, either for their beauty or their hideousness. Hell has a special subdivision for L.A. architects who massacre a neighborhood, ignore its character, and ruin its scale. One house at a time, they are eliminating the 1950s. They erect oversized, six-bedroom homes where a nice three-bedroom ranch formerly rested. To me, such castles are the architectural equivalent of porn.

Nothing against porn, of course.

Every week, it seems another old house has been scraped from its lot, and some new monstrosity is rising from the dust, a Ramada-like estate that stretches from the very edge of one property line to the very edge of the next. Dryer vents blow from one house right into the next. I mean, what's the point of having a large property if you can't enclose and air-condition it?

Up one street and down the next I go, then over the horse trails, where I rarely see horses. From there, I spy the preening backyards of L.A.'s landed gentry—attorneys and executives, producers and directors. Gardeners tend these places, of course, clip them tight and clean the dog poop. Each morning, the Weed Eaters descend like swarms of insects. They leave behind gardens and lawns that are soft, pretty as a Monet.

There is much to admire here, much to covet. For instance, there is one new Colonial, white like a wedding cake, that I have been flirting with for more than 3 years now. It is the sort of home no one ever tears down, the sort of home that stands for centuries.

Thing is, for 3 years I have trotted by this dream house and spotted not a single soul fetching a newspaper or climbing into a car. There are no toys scattered in the backyard, the way toys should be. People live there— I saw the moving van when they arrived—yet there is not one sign of life. If we moved in—just showed up one day with our scooters and our plastic golf clubs, our horseshoes and our tomato cages—I wonder if the owners would even notice.

I head back up the hill to the busy streets, where frantic mothers risk life and limb to get their children to school on time. The mothers in our town are notorious for their aggressive-distracted driving habits, balancing the checkbook at lights or filling out some permission slip while zooming down the boulevard.

I spot one mother in a minivan, inexplicably driving the speed limit, who is being nearly goosed by a giant SUV that is riding her bumper at 30 miles per hour. This is not an isolated incident. Around here, mothers get goosed all the time.

Such tailgating tactics make me sympathetic to the mother in the minivan, till she suddenly veers—without signaling—and scoots up a side street, nearly causing the SUV to burrow up her tailpipe.

I fear for the mothers of my fair town. They have not an easy life. Calendars full, they must drive with cell phones to their ears and giant vats of Starbucks on their perfumed laps. Occasionally, you see them applying mascara while entering a school zone. No wonder they seldom signal. No wonder they take wide, sweeping, too-fast turns that remind me of cruise ships fleeing typhoons.

"I'm late for school!" the desperate housewives scream. "Don't you realize how hard this all is?"

Now it's nearly nightfall. I am coaching third base, which is no place for a brooding existentialist. Between complex thoughts, I try to get the attention of the base runner on second, a promising but moody cello player named Brittany.

"Come on, Brittany," I yell, before realizing that the entire team is named Brittany, including several of the mothers.

At the end of the day, we have softball like this. It is as close as we really come to Happy Hour.

It used to be even happier here at Happy Hour. A year or two ago, the mothers used to bring giant coolers full of cold refreshing beverages. After two or three of these beverages, the parents often forgot that there was a game going on at all or why they were even here or that they even had daughters. Complaints were few, and morale was high. Indeed, we had some of the happiest moms on Earth.

"Run, Kelsey, run!" a mother would scream.

"Which one's Kelsey?" another mother would ask.

"Um, the little blond," the first mother would explain. "I think she's your daughter."

"Oh, yeah. Run, Kelsey, run!"

One by one, little girls would come to the plate on martini-glass legs, practicing the sweeping, ineffective uppercuts their fathers taught them. Between pitches, they'd stand perfectly still, paralyzed with fear or acid reflux. In softball, two things can happen, both of them bad. You can strike out, or you can get a hit. If you strike out, the parents call out patronizing things like "good try" or "that's all right, honey; you'll do better next time." If you get a hit, you move on to a base, where more bad things await.

While I coached the kids on such subtleties of the game, the parents would sit in the stands, sipping their refreshments and relaxing at the end of the day. I envied these spectator parents for their leisure time, their mild quips. Their irreverence. In little snippets, I'd hear them grow gradually more daring, while discussing some of the bigger issues of the day, such as:

- Do lobsters suffer when you steam them?
- What's your favorite gin?
- Who do you have your car insurance with?
- Does this look infected?
- God, I love your ass (a sign that the tequila may have finally taken hold).

One game, I think it was a Friday, the parents were in such a state of euphoria, so thrilled by their talk of home equity, school test scores, and who'd been Botoxed that week, that they created a din that actually bothered the players on the field and affected their caliber of play, such that it was.

"Salsa?" I heard one mother ask as she nearly fell into a buffet of light hors d'oeuvres.

"Or is that humus?"

"Yes."

"Gimme some of that humus."

The conviviality was overwhelming, like the Daytona Beach of their youth. Each inning, the parents grew a little louder, a little younger. Here the parents were, out trying to be supportive of their kids, and they were having more fun than the children.

For the kids, it was odd to be so ignored. All their lives, these parents were breathing down their necks about this or about that. Now they seemed so disinterested. So . . . happy?

"Could you hold it down over there?" I called from the dugout.

"Yeah, hold it down," echoed my assistant.

"Oh, bite me," came a voice from the back row. Everybody laughed.

A few minutes later, the team parents brought us tiny cups of refreshments, hoping to win over the coaching staff and keep their daughters high in the lineup. Pretty wives in capri pants would tiptoe onto the infield between outs and discreetly hand the base coach 2 ounces of slushy margarita that had been shaken and stirred as it jounced along in the back of a Lincoln Navigator on the way over. We always declined, of course, unless the game was against Miller's team, which we considered the Evil Empire of little girl softball. They weren't. But that's what everybody thought.

"Beat 'em," the pretty mother would say with a wink and hand us a plastic cup.

"Um, I can't take this. I'm coaching," we'd remind them.

Then we'd look over at Coach Miller, working the umpire and trying for every little advantage he could get. In little girl softball, the margins for such things are very slim.

"Give me that," we'd say, grab the cup and down the slushy tequila in one over-limed gulp.

Now, wisely, our league prohibits such adult-friendly refreshments, and the spectators sit calmly, bent over in the bleachers, almost mournful. From the side, they look like a bleacher filled with parentheses. Spines curving. A chiropractor's fever dream.

"Why doesn't your husband," a mother asks my wife, "stay in the nice white coach's box that Mr. Parker drew for him?"

"He's just like that," I hear my wife say.

Now that they are sober again, the mothers are more tuned in to the nuances of the game: namely that their daughters actually get to bat and occasionally make a defensive play in the field. They fix their bright, pretty, halogen eyes on the field and barely blink.

"Run, Megan, run!" they scream.

"Foul ball!" the umpire screams.

"Run, Megan!"

"It was foul," someone explains.

"So?"

So? We're the kind of team that's not that picky. We run on foul balls and fair ones, too. We sit in the bleachers and in the dugouts on the sweetest April days you'd ever imagine and watch the sun drop below the tree line, till it's evening in the 'hood. A full day. A simple life. Is this any way to run a suburb? Listen to the inmates.

"Nice hit, Emily!" a mother screams through cupped hands.

"That was Caitlin," another parent explains.

"Nice hit whoever you are," they say with a laugh.

Such tiny moments, stacked one atop the other, make up our suburban lives. There's nothing to be too ashamed of here. Nor much of anything to brag about, really. Each day, the same little song plays over and over—carpool, school, softball, bed—the soundtrack to the American Dream.

I sing it happily, if a tad out of tune.

Like a father, goosed.

2

PARDON OUR LUST

SO HERE WE ARE on the couch late at night, surreptitiously watching a racy movie in a house full of children, who were produced by the very sexual tension that we are trying to maintain here in a 20-year marriage. Your marriage hasn't had its ups and downs? Who you kidding?

The two younger children are sleeping. The two older ones are out with friends. At any moment, one of them could burst in on us sitting on the couch, sipping Trader Joe's Chardonnay and trying not to fall asleep too soon on a Saturday night. As you know, long-term love can be very tiring.

On the screen, *Haunting Desires* is playing. In essence, it's a romance, in that it involves people wooing other people against improbable odds. From what I can tell, some of the people are vampires and some of them are not. But when the people who are not vampires hook up with the vampires, they become vampires. It's sort of like dating the Irish. After a while, you just become one of them.

"So how can I fulfill your every desire?" the vampire asks.

"That would be a pretty tall order," says the mortal.

I never claimed it was Ingmar Bergman's best work, though many of the scenes are quite dark and, I'm sure, loaded with a sulking symbolism.

As any dad will tell you, there is an art to watching a nudie scene. First, you try to determine whether the breasts are real. Then you look for any sign of actual chemistry between the actors, because that's what porn's all about really, romance. In my mind, Freud had it backward: Sex is really just an excuse to fall in love.

"What do you want?" the mortal whispers.

"To set you free to be the kind of person you want to be," growls the vampire.

As with a lot of soft-core porn, the second act is a little slow. I begin to notice that the vampires often skip foreplay of any kind. They just sort of stand around in the shadows till the young maiden prepares for bed. The vampires' eyes turn green, and then they pounce. It is a mating ritual not unlike frogs and other amphibians.

The maidens, of course, welcome the fact that some monster has just jumped out from the dark to ravish them. They don't even seem to mind the bad dental work on several of the vampires, or that the main vampire is perhaps 20 pounds overweight and could use a decent haircut. When I skip foreplay myself, which is every time, I am either slapped or scolded. But vampires seem to get away with it repeatedly.

Now the vampire is wrapping his arms around the maiden's slender legs and jerking her fetching rear end into the air, I think to show his strength, which with vampires is considerable, even the out-of-shape ones. Vampires almost never exercise, and their diet consists almost entirely of fast food and virgins. Yet these vampires are as strong as ten Schwarzeneggers. There he is tearing her shirt and . . .

"Mommy?"

The "Mommy" call comes from the little girl's bedroom, prompting my wife to dive into the couch in search of the remote control to turn off this adult fare. There is the strong belief among married people that, despite the fact that they are married, if it is ever revealed to the children that they have sexual urges, God will reach down and crush them. At least that's the sense I get.

"Mommyyyyyyyyyyyyy?"

My wife, still fully clothed, of course, is searching frantically for the remote control so she can turn off *Haunting Desires* before the little girl climbs out of bed and walks into the room. In her haste, my wife has half-fallen off the couch, so that she has to thrust her foot to the wood floor in order to catch herself. This sends a sonic boom across the wooden under-carriage of the house and alarms the little girl even more.

"Mommy, what's that noise?"

My wife goes to comfort our daughter, get her a glass of water, and soothe her back to sleep. Of course, as any father knows, this means that the overextended mother soon falls asleep as well, leaving me to ponder vampire love alone.

It wasn't always so.

When my wife and I first met, love posed no obstacles. We were children ourselves really, just done with college. I was a Florida sportswriter. She was an assistant food editor. Believe me, it was even sexier than it sounds.

I knew it was serious when I got nervous before calling her. In advance of dates, I'd drive to restaurants to be sure they were okay and that I carried enough cash to cover. I was behaving completely abnormally, which is to say decently and with a dose of maturity. It was as if I was suddenly contemplating the priesthood, and I wanted to do well before the eyes of God.

I should've seen the warning signs. Despite the fact that she was unbelievably sexy, I wasn't even imaging her in uncompromising positions, as I usually did with the 21-year-old women I'd meet. Instead, I imagined her holding a bouquet of daffodils and singing like Julie Andrews, her lovely and considerable chest wrapped in that vest that Julie once wore. The hills were alive, and so was I.

Our courtship wasn't without complication. There was a guy in a Jeep who wouldn't go away. Wait, that was me. Then there was another guy, in a little Volkswagen bug, who also wouldn't go away. His name was Spam. Or Dan. Or Gary. Who cares? Neither of us would go away. We never spoke. I fantasized about killing him with my Excalibur. Freud could've had a field day with that one.

In the end, I stole his beautiful girl and never looked back. We escaped to New Orleans, where relationships go to die, mostly from temptation. Ours nearly did, but then suddenly there were two children, both as pretty as her, and what kind of fool forsakes all that? Lord help me: I was now smitten three times, 'stead of once.

Our social life was spent with other young couples. We'd meet at their house or ours and spend the first hour discussing how exhausting it was to be the eager parents of young children. Over wine, we convinced ourselves that we were the most exhausted parents ever—the first generation to ever experience such weariness—and that children were different now, more demanding.

"Exhausting doesn't even cover it," one mother explained.

"No, exhausting isn't even the right word."

It's a long life, but we didn't know that then. We busied ourselves with fixing up the only houses we could afford. We rushed at home repair projects, as if going to battle, then compared war stories on the weekend. Shared power tools. Admired our wives' slim tanned legs.

One day, my wife and I found a sad-sack old Victorian in such disrepair that potential babysitters all thought it was haunted.

"It looks," the sitter would say, "like that *Nightmare on Elm Street* house."

"It does?"

I was actually pretty proud of the big old house. It had 12 rooms and four fireplaces. I never dreamed we could own such a palace, even if the plumbing dated from the 15th century.

"That was just a movie," my wife assured the babysitter.

"I've got homework," the sitter lied.

So in an effort to attract a babysitter, if nothing else, we worked to make the house presentable again. We would spend long, hard hours on things people would never see: shoring up floors, running vents to the water heater. That sort of work took 3 years. Then we turned to painting and refinishing floors—easy tasks, really.

To refinish a 150-year-old cypress floor, you merely had to rent a quarter-ton machine that operated like a lawnmower on meth. You'd wrap giant sheets of sandpaper around its drum, inadvertently sanding your hands in the process and removing the little channels in your fingers that comprise your fingerprints. Each room took 2 days and several layers of fingertips. As we worked, we were erasing legal proof of our own identities.

They were the longest days of our lives. At night, we'd fall asleep to Garrison Keillor talking about Lutheran weddings on PBS. It was a blissful exhaustion. In our spare time, we took care of two kids.

They were getting older by then, 3 and 6. They helped with the renovation by spackling my shoes while I worked.

"There, Daddy," my daughter would say.

"Thanks, honey."

"Now the other shoe," she'd say.

When the home was finished, we moved. Just 30, we'd decided it was then or never, so we took the job offer in Los Angeles, where the homes were a quarter the size and four times the price. It seemed like a smart move at the time.

"You really want to go to L.A.?" our friends all asked.

We left New Orleans while friends stood in the yard and waved. There was the gay couple next door, Rick and Wayne, good as neighbors get. There was Rene and Don from down the block, whose kids were the same ages as ours. They all stood there in the yard, wondering what friends have wondered for centuries: Why leave such a pleasant, soothing, afford-able place to live in that sewer by the sea? Why California?

All we knew was that we were too young to settle down. Wanderlust is an American virtue. It had been good to us so far, so why not again? Didn't the world belong to those who took risks? Besides, Louisiana sum-mers are like bowls of very hot soup.

In Los Angeles, we rented a while. That's what you do in L.A., you rent first so you can study the market and discover that the only things you can afford are doghouses and empty appliance boxes. Our newest friends, a young family just arrived from Houston, had bought a cozy two-bed-room on a dull street in Burbank for $250,000. We were envious as hell. Also demoralized. We could never afford $250,000.

But we stuck it out, told ourselves that we were building up my resume if nothing else, while making our school teacher landlords rich. We also did what cash-strapped young couples always seem to do in times of duress: We had another baby.

She arrived like a rainstorm on an April day. We put her in the old crib in our bedroom and slept on eggshells so as not to wake her.

High rent quickly soaked up any money we'd made on the New Orleans house, so my wife went back to work. As is the tradition, the extra money she made went mostly to child care.

On the weekends, I coached T-ball, and my wife scoured the San

Fernando Valley for any little house we might afford. We'd heard that some neighbors had bought up in the hills, where the schools were better. On the way to an open house, we stumbled upon something. It was becoming increasingly clear that, for us, stumbling upon things was really working out.

"Come on in," the real estate agent said.

It was a contemporary place, the kind I loathed. No moldings. Aluminum windows. A garage dominating the entrance like a big wart. Still, I'd have given my left arm and probably a testicle to have a good-sized place like this.

"Well, this one's going for $450,000," the agent said.

Ugh.

"But there is a place next door . . ." the agent said.

The place next door was a dump. Like half the homes in America, it was built in the mid-'50s. It had three bedrooms when we needed four. It had a funky rock roof. But out back was a wall of olive trees instead of the usual parched patch of grass that most L.A. starter homes offered. It soon became clear that I wasn't buying the house, I was buying 20 olive trees. Think of the martinis we could make.

"I like the yard," I told my wife.

"It's too steep," she warned.

"The kitchen is cool," I said.

"The kitchen's a mess."

"The schools are great," I reminded her. "And we could always add on."

The prospect of more renovation didn't exactly arouse her. In New Orleans, it had almost cost us our marriage.

"What's that noise?" I asked the agent.

"The freeway," she said

"God, it's close," I said

"Some agents will tell you it sounds like the ocean," she said.

I loved the beauty of that. The agent was trying to tell us to think of freeway noise as Pacific surf without coming right out and making the ridiculous statement that a freeway could sound like an ocean. What it sounded like was trucks and cars.

"Hear that, honey?" I asked.

"What?"

"That's the ocean," I said.

"No, it's not."

"We'll take it," I told the agent.

In the basement, we found a stash of porn. The sellers had included all contents with the house, so this porn didn't even cost us an extra penny.

"Oh, look at this one," the cute young real estate agent giggled.

"Okay," I said, examining the videotape's box.

"Oh, look at *this* one," giggled my wife.

It was easily the best part of the buying process, sifting through porn tapes in the cramped basement with the cute young agent and my cute young wife. It was almost like a moment in a porn tape itself, and I'd be lying if I said my imagination didn't spike. Any second, I expected them to start undressing each other. This was California, after all.

"Ewwwww," I heard my wife say, breaking the mood.

"This stuff is dis-*gust*-ing," the agent said with a scowl.

It was then that I realized that life is not a porn movie. It's rarely even rated R.

"Oh my god, I can't look at this stuff," my wife said.

"Let me see," the agent said.

"Ewwwwwwwwwww!!!" they both squealed.

A week later, my wife told me that I'd be relieved to know that the junk man had hauled away everything in the basement, except some tools she thought I'd like.

"What about those, you know, tapes?" I asked.

"Oh, we threw those out, too," my wife said.

"Thank God," I said.

"I know you're disappointed," she teased.

No, not at all. I was grateful to be rid of them. If the junk man did indeed haul the tapes to the landfill, more power to him. There's no place for stuff like that around a family home.

But occasionally . . .

"Honey?"

"Huh?"

"You coming to bed?"

It is midnight now, well after most suburbs close down. The vampire movie I found on Cinemax is over. I take a last swig of wine, click off the TV, and look for my wife, who I find snoring softly on our daughter's bed. As most men know, even the sexiest, most beautiful women in the world snore a little. I find the sound incredibly alluring.

"Honey?"

No answer.

"You coming to bed?"

Nothing.

Somehow, we had four children.

3

Kids Ruin Everything

CHILDREN. Yes, we had four of them. We keep having them, for no apparent purpose and in no discernible pattern. One came along, then a few years later, yet another. The third followed in 5 years—surprise!—and then the fourth 12 years after that. Oops. They're sort of like bad hurricanes. You go along for a while without one and start to think, "Hey, hurricanes aren't so bad," and then *wham*, there goes the boathouse.

We use, apparently, the same birth control methods preferred by hillbillies: whiskey and religion. Before being intimate, my wife slugs down an ounce of Jack Daniel's and then prays, "Please, God, not another kid. At least not with this goober." I merely sit near by, plucking my banjo, remembering how lucky I am.

"Kids ruin everything," another father recently said, and I knew immediately that he meant it in jest. I think he meant it in jest. Wouldn't he have meant it in jest?

Because children are just puppies with bigger brains. They ruin the floors and carpets, walls and woodwork. They crap up the car and your social life and your vacations. They futz with your stereo and your photo albums and leave their fingerprints on the newly varnished cabinets. They soak up all your free time, ambush your marriage, and compromise your soul.

Still, for reasons that are somewhat unclear, I love my kids shamelessly. I love them in ways they will never understand nor appreciate. I love them for the outlandish statements they make and the way they argue with me on politics, music, and how to play a bunt down the third base line. Nothing they could ever do could make me love them less. That doesn't stop them from trying, of course.

"Dad?"

"Huh?"

"Can I have some money?" the boy asks.

"Of course," I say.

"Thanks," he says.

We stand there watching each other, waiting for the other guy to make the first move. He's waiting for me to reach for my wallet. I'm waiting for him to justify this request. We're two gunslingers, wondering if we heard the other guy correctly.

"Dad?"

"Huh?"

"Can I have some money?"

I'd like to think that they love me unconditionally, when in fact they love me in proportion to the amount of spending money they receive in any given week. There's nothing wrong with buying love, of course. It happens all the time. The important thing to remember is to get something in return. A handshake and a hug. A receipt, at the very least.

"How much do you need?" I ask the boy.

"Twenty?" he says.

"That's all?" I say.

"I don't want to be greedy," he explains.

"Good for you," I say proudly.

The boy goes through cash the way the colonel goes through chicken. So I explain to the teenager that in return for the 20 bucks, I'd like to see him rake the front yard till noon. Notice how I attach a minimum amount of time for the task? Had I failed to do that, I'm pretty sure he'd rake one leaf then call it a day. "Whew, that was some big leaf," he'd tell himself. "I might've pulled a muscle."

It's the new American work ethic—work a little, then spend the rest of the time figuring out how to scam the boss. In most cases, I salute this ethic. I appreciate it in everyone but my own children.

"It's a deal," he says after I explain the raking offer.

"Good," I say.

"Can I do it when I get back?"

"Sure," I say. "If I can pay you when you get back."

"Daaaaaaaaaaaaaad!"

That's "dad," sung by a desperate person. Rhymes with "bad."

"Daaaaaaaaaaaaaad!" I hear another voice say.

It's his attorney. She's 13 and lives with us. I think she's related because when she gets really upset, the tips of her ears turn pink as cotton candy. Just like her mother's. You know the type.

"Dad, that's not fair," she says.

"It's not?"

"Can't you just give him the money now?" she asks.

"No."

"He needs to go now," she explains, "or he'll be late."

"For what?"

"What will you be late for?" she whispers to her big brother.

"I'm getting Starbucks with Matt," he tells her.

"He's getting Starbucks with Matt," she says.

I had no idea he was so pressed for time. Nor did I know that he needed the money for such an important meeting: Starbucks with Matt. My boy and his attorney should've been more forthright with their request. The legal profession isn't what it used to be. Still, I hold my ground.

"The rake's out back," I say.

The thing about kids is that they're all different. They can come from the same gene pool and the same environment and still turn out as different as snow peas and fudge.

From what I hear, though, there are certain basic guidelines for parenting, underlying fundamentals that lead to good results:

- Set some rules.
- Stand your ground.
- When they screw up, make sure there are consequences.
- Pour yourself a whiskey, say a prayer, and put your hands over both ears so your brains don't spill out from all the yelling.

Those are the guidelines that I hear about often, anyway. A lot of parents buy into it, too. Some boast excellent results. Basically, parenting is like deep sea fishing, except the fights last longer and the smells are entirely different.

"Daaaaaaaaaaaad!" the boy wails.

"Hey, how about those Dodgers," I say, turning back to the paper.

I love a stubborn dad. I watch others in action and think, "You go, guy! Keep their little butts in line! Give 'em hell, Harry."

When I was a younger father—and the other dads, too—we were convinced we could create mini-democracies at home, with equal participation and a flattened hierarchy of authority. No one would need to yell or issue ultimatums. The little dears would respond out of the goodness of their hearts and an inherent sense of justice. No spanking. No stern threats. Heck, we could do away with the traditional concept of dad and mom as despots. Like the Marx Brothers, we'd all be more or less equal.

It worked. Till they turned 2.

Now, instead, my wife and I step forward and try to run the house. It's an audacious philosophy, that parents should be in charge. That kids must do what they're told or face some sort of stinging rebuke.

This goes against everything kids teach each other. That the world revolves around them and that they should run the home. Basically, kids believe in three principals of childhood. Essentially, they are:

- Give-me, give-me, give-me.
- Now, give-me some more.
- If you don't give me what I want, I'll tune you out and never speak to you again.

Like the parental guidelines, these also have had mixed results. Most parents don't give-give-give. Some have, but they're gone now; they collapsed and died from lack of gratitude. Instead, good parents are demanding something in return. Respect. Love. Chores.

"I don't have time to rake now," the boy explains, calmer now, trying to wear me down. If you're a parent, you may have experienced this tactic.

"He doesn't have time," his attorney says.

"I understand," I say.

"You do?" they both say, surprised.

22

"Yeah, because I don't have time to pay you," I say.

For a while, we adopted the Euro. My wife and I thought that by switching to another currency, we could start all over and thereby establish the fee-for-work ethic that the kids were struggling with. They think money comes from ATM machines, not work. Their entire lives, they have seen mothers pull up to ATMs and withdraw 100 bucks like it was nothing. God bless America, they thought. Why can't the Third World get some of these?

Then one day their mother patiently explained that you can't take money out of an ATM unless you've put money into one first. This mystified them, because as far as they could tell, they had never witnessed anyone actually putting money into an ATM. To them, it would be like putting ketchup back into the ketchup bottle. Of course, you could do it. But why would you?

Eventually, our experiment with the Euro failed, and we returned to using the U.S. dollar. I resorted to teaching economics at breakfast and dinner, the main message being the value of a dollar. You reap what you sow. Money doesn't grow on trees, you know.

"Does it grow on bushes?" my lovely and patient older daughter asked.

"No," I said.

"Does it grow in gardens?" the boy asked.

"No."

"Then where does it grow?" the older daughter asked.

"Don't be a wise guy," I said.

"Daddy, what's *sow* mean?" the little girl asked, eager to reap as much as possible.

"Suck-up," said her brother.

My lesson plan also included chores, which were an entirely foreign concept to them. Sure, they'd made their beds and fed the dogs. But real work? For kids? Didn't that go out of style with, like, Dickens?"

The lessons, held on Saturday mornings, started with the very basics.

"This," I'd say, "is a broom."

"Slow down, Dad," the boy said.

"Yeah, I'm trying to take notes," said the older daughter.

"Keep going, Dad, I'm listening," said the little red-haired girl.

"Suck-up," growled her brother.

As with most children, I found that you could not just hand them a broom and point them to a pile of dust. You had to actually show them how to wrap their dirty fingers around the broom handle, then, as if giving ballroom dance lessons, demonstrate the sweeping motion most commonly associated with cleaning up. Without such detailed instructions, they would use the brooms to ride around the garage like witches after too many margaritas, chasing each other and casting spells against their younger, more sober siblings. All sorts of threats involving warts and trolls, drawbridges and lost love.

"Daddy?"

"Huh?"

"Am I going to marry a troll?" the little girl asked after one such session.

"Only if he comes from money," I explained.

"Good," she said and skipped back to the garage.

It didn't stop with brooms. You'd have to discuss dust pan techniques and how to sweep something up without leaving little corn rows of dust that would later get tracked into the house. They learned to be relentless with a broom, what a cobweb was, how to scream at spiders to get them to leave the garage. Shrilly yelling at insects played right into many of their natural gifts.

"Get out, you stupid spider!!!" they'd scream, an aria of fear and hatred. "Get OUUUUUUUT!"

Soon—it took only 6 or 7 years, really—the kids began to get the hang of doing chores for money. But they had trouble with the concept that the chore came first, and then the money. They attempted to obtain cash advances by using chore credit.

Which brings us right back to today's standoff.

"Dad, can I have some money?" the boy asks.

I love them completely. I love the way they try to eat linguini with an iced tea spoon or oatmeal with a fork. I love the way they order beef and broccoli at the Chinese joint, and then methodically shove aside all the broccoli to eat only the beef.

I love the way they bang their schoolbooks against the walls and leave their handprints in the hallway. The way they twirl their hair at dinner even after their mother scolds them. The way they jump when you catch them squirting Reddi-Wip directly into their mouths in front of the fridge.

I love them for their developing sense of decency. Their kindness. Their restraint.

"MOM!" one of them screams from three rooms away.

"Don't yell," their mother says, calmly.

"MOMMMMMM!"

"What? What?"

"I just wanted to make sure you were here," they explain.

She always is. And so am I. We love them in ways that defy all explanation. And, really, they haven't ruined a thing.

$\underline{4}$

A LITTLE NOTE TO THE TODDLER

WE WENT OUT the other day, you and I. You were probably too small to remember it, so I'm jotting down a few notes here to remind you as you get older and wonder what kind of father your old man was and what life was like when you were very small.

We spent this particular day at the beach, one of your absolute favorite play spots, given as it is to partial nudity and creamy back rubs. You can yell as loud as you like at the beach, which you did. Those handprints you're always leaving on the kitchen walls aren't a problem here. When you spill food, which you always do, a gull swoops in to eat it.

As the tide came in, we danced in the waves a while. I held your hand too firmly. We've lost a lot of things to the Pacific Ocean—buckets, sandals, sunglasses—but I was determined that you would not be one of them. You ran at the water as if on fire.

Let me describe you as you are on this day: You are 2. You have your mother's big brown eyes and skin like fresh pie. Your hair is straight and shiny as a doll's. I think it might be nylon.

You are also almost frightfully thin, with ribbing like an old lifeguard boat. There's this ballplayer named Randy Johnson. They call him the "Big Unit." I call you the "Little Unit." As in, "Here comes a wave, Little Unit. Hold on."

You don't talk so well yet. You remind me of one of those Chicago politicians who speaks as if he has a mouthful of walnuts. You slur your vowels, swallow your consonants. "Th" sounds come out all slushy.

But you and I still communicate like twins in the womb. With nudges. Smirks. Laughter. The Earth is our ally. Adventure is our friend. After 30 minutes in the Santa Monica sand, you were breaded as a fish stick.

"Da!" you yelled.

"Whataya mean by that?" I asked, then chased you down the beach.

It is a nice body of water, the Pacific. A chilly, churning pool that kicks its tonic-water mist into the dry mountain air. What sets your home state apart from others is this combo of cool oceans and dry mountain air. All afternoon, you were back lit by the same California sun that made stars of Redford and Streep. Wish I'd brought a camera. There are no words for the play of light on a 2-year-old's chubby profile.

After a couple of hours, I wanted to leave to walk along a nearby promenade. This was not okay with you. It was growing chilly but you wanted to splash and play till the moon arrived and the sea birds settled along the shore for the evening. You were stubborn, but you were never unpleasant. As we left, you helped pick up your beach toys and place them in the yellow mesh bag.

We made the long trek to the car, which was parked out on the heavily timbered pier. The car was warm from sitting in the sun. Putting you in the back was like placing you in an incubator to warm you. Fearlessly, I changed your diaper. You kicked. You laughed. I wiped you down with the beach towel. Sand was in your every crevice. You seemed to like that.

We discovered about then that we hadn't packed an extra pair of dry pants for you. So I dressed you in a gray fleece sweatshirt that fit you like a mini-dress, then placed you in the stroller. If there's anyplace where you can go out for a walk without pants, it's Santa Monica, California. We headed east.

They have this promenade along Third Street, where vendors set up little carts and street musicians perform for money. The place was full of guitar players—California produces them like palm trees—and we stopped to listen. Several of them were very good. It seemed to bother you that no one else was stopping to listen to these very good guitar players. It seemed rude to you, a 2-year-old, that people would just walk by. Rude? You ain't seen nothin'. Just wait till you reach the first grade.

We strolled along the promenade for about an hour. It was a show, let me tell you. There was one woman in a skin-tight dress carrying a very small dog. She wasn't a person; she was an event. Best of all, she was wearing even less than you were, which took a lot of the attention away from your own misdemeanor.

There were rich society matrons and young actor types. But that's okay. They didn't really bother us. Aspiring actors always look frightening—skinny and a little psychotic—but they are harmless really. One had a script under her arm and was mouthing bad dialogue. It was like being amid a bunch of hip, harmless schizophrenics.

We stopped for a slice of cheese pizza. You grabbed it from my hand like you had never eaten before. "Your mother will be so happy," I told you. You didn't answer. At the next table, lovers leaned on their elbows, losing themselves in each other. You smiled at them and ate your crust.

On the way back, a bum talked to us about something that didn't make any sense. It was sort of like being in the office, except I didn't have to stand there and nod politely. A car paused at a light to let us cross. I know these are small things, but some day maybe these details will bring it back to you. The sun fell toward the water as if in need of a drink.

You wanted to go on the amusement rides that dot the pier, but I pulled you toward the fisherman. You hail from a tribe of Irish fisherman who—to hear their offspring tell it—never caught a single fish. So they came to America to work in the bars and the hotels. Let that be a lesson to you. Leave the halibut be. Trend yourself toward indoor work.

Indeed, none of the fishermen we saw this day had caught a thing either. Of course, as you'll learn, catching something from the water is a fluke. Trust me. Given your genes, your best bet is wine and cheese.

At the far end of the pier, we watched the dolphins play and the ocean sparkle like a sequined gown. A sailboat carved the space between us and Catalina. We caught a couple of rides, including the Ferris wheel. I am afraid of almost nothing except heights and Ben Affleck movies. As our carriage leapt over the top, I held you and the handrail. My heart was in my forehead.

You seemed to enjoy the view. We could see all the way to Malibu to the north and the Palos Verdes Peninsula to the south. I'll say this about your birthplace: from 5 p.m. to nightfall, there is no prettier sight in the world than its oceanfront.

Time for dinner, so we sought out a hot dog. As we headed for a restaurant, we came across an old hippie with a bubble machine perched on the pier. Like magic, the bubbles poured out by the hundreds. You ran through them, giggling. The hippie tried to talk to you, but you would have none of that. As you left, you handed him a dollar.

We ditched your stroller and walked along the strand, where the Rollerbladers and joggers go. You walked 10 feet behind me, like a drunk in a parade. You waved to strangers. You tongue-kissed a golden retriever. You smiled at pigeons. In all of nature, it's the pigeons you like the best.

We found a little place that sold hot dogs, fries, and lemonade; that's all. You dipped your fries in mustard then ate them. Much of the mustard landed on your face. For a while, I was afraid a gull might get you, mistake you for a giant french fry and carry you off to dinner. Didn't happen. Nearby, volleyball players fell to the sand.

After dinner, we tried the swings along Muscle Beach. You love to swing. Except for playing in the waves, it may be your favorite thing. These swings in particular were nice because, when you swung forward, it seemed as though you were being launched into the ocean, which was darker blue now, the color of new jeans.

Back home, I washed you. Even after 20 minutes in the bath, you still had sand in the creases where your legs meet your butt. I fear that from this day forward, you will always carry one or two grains of sand from this trip—in your scalp, in your private areas. Like gold dust on a miner.

We ended the day with a book, *Goodnight Moon*, a classic by Margaret Wise Brown. I wouldn't recommend it to everyone. I found it short on character development, and the transitions are rather abrupt. Basically, it's about a little bunny saying good night to all the items around him. How insipid is that? It held my attention for, like, 2 seconds.

But you really seemed to enjoy it. You're at that age where you like to read the same book 100 times, till the pages are torn and my thumbprints have burrowed into the bindings. To you, familiarity is comfort. Reading the same book a hundred times creates the sort of warmth I get from double-malt scotch.

So you put your head on my shoulder and we read *Goodnight Moon*.

As we turned the pages, you seemed to identify more and more with the young bunny. I'm just guessing, but I assume you saw the bunny as a Messiah figure and the moon as God. Like I said, it's just my interpretation, based on the reflection I saw in your almond eyes.

> *"In the great green room,*
> *There was a telephone*
> *And a red balloon,*
> *And a picture of –*
> *The cow jumping over the moon."*

Goodnight, moon. Goodnight, Little Unit.

5

THE DOG WITH THE DEFECTIVE FANNY

THERE'S A BEAGLE in my bed. It's 7 a.m. on a Saturday, and from the dog's soft intestinal sounds, you'd think there was coffee brewing in his colon. Maybe that's just wishful thinking, but that's what it sounds like: coffee brewing. Hiss. Drip. Hiss. Drip. Hiss.

The little beagle puppy is barely a year. He's not mine. Legally, he belongs to my lovely and patient older daughter. I guess that would make him my granddog.

Like most granddogs, he gets away with more than a regular dog would. For instance, right now his fanny is on my pillow, facing me. The beagle has some serious head-fanny issues, namely the inability to distinguish which end is his head and which end is his fanny. With his fanny in my face—cheek to cheek, so to speak—he thinks he is sleeping properly and showing me the utmost respect. What he is really doing is showing me his very hairy tush.

"Can you," I call out to my daughter, "get your dog's butt out of my face?"

"But he loves you," she explains.

All love is not equal. Nor is it inherently good. When I made the decision to share my bed, it was to allow our own dog—a dear cocker spaniel—under the covers, where he sleeps like 20 pounds of warm coal at my feet on winter nights. During the summer, he beds down in my easy chair in the den, for him a cooler crib. It's a seasonal marriage, and a very good one, proving that dog love is a powerful emotion, especially for a middle-aged man.

Then along comes this love-struck beagle, and now the pets-in-bed decision seems like a bad one. First, he has allergies and will occasionally begin a snorting fit in the middle of the night that sounds like a barn full of asthmatic hogs. These usually pass in 10 or 15 minutes, just long enough to completely wake the house.

"It's all right," says my wife while petting the beagle's head, certain that like most maladies in our family, it's mostly psychological.

"Just calm down and go back to sleep," she tells him.

"Christ, what's wrong with him?" I grumble.

"Just go back to sleep," she tells me, too, and I fall back asleep to the slurpy sounds of a little beagle licking himself.

Then there is the fact that he can sense those rare times my wife and I have a chance to be intimate. He seems tuned in to romance and passion and attempts to snuff it out with his wet little beagle nose. More often than not, he's successful. Had we this dog when we were first married, we might right now be childless.

But mostly there is the issue of the dog not knowing which end is his head and which is his fanny. Imagine going through life like that? You'd be doomed to careers in Congress or hosting postgame highlights on ESPN.

"Nice to meet you, Congressman," your constituents would say. "I'd recognize that hairy smile anywhere."

Down near my stomach, the beagle sneezes. In his little beagle brain, he's probably wondering why I'm sleeping with my ass on the pillow. Beagles tend to work that way. They always assume it's the other guy who's confused.

"He really does love you," says my wife, standing at the doorway.

"Yeah, Dad," my daughter says. "He thinks you're Grandpa."

They are standing at the bedroom door admiring the beagle's position on the pillow. They think it's cute the way this dog has wormed his way into my otherwise charmed and pampered life.

"Just think of him as Snoopy," my wife says, perhaps forgetting what a snide, undermining anarchist Snoopy could be.

"He's more like Marmaduke," says my daughter.

She bought him sight unseen from a puppy mill in the Deep South. They shipped him to California in a tiny crate, I assume from some former Confederate prison with dysentery still in the water supply. Confederate prisons were notorious for their bad plumbing and sanitation. Most likely, the puppy lapped up a few infectious diseases, and then came to share them with us.

When he arrived, he wasn't a dog, he was more like a slipper. The kids would take him to the park, where he seduced large crowds of people, including me. We needed a puppy in our house like we needed another termite. But I'm a sucker for things more helpless than I am. How much trouble could a little slipper be?

In a week, he'd ruined the bedroom carpet and had started in on our new oak floors. Turned out he wasn't a slipper, but a watering can. He'd also begun to claw-shred the doors and the weather stripping around them. It was his attempt, I assume, at recreating his former moonshine and NASCAR surroundings in rural Alabama.

The puppy grew quickly. He belonged to my college-aged daughter, but as can often happen, the dog soon became my dog, too. Back from college, he'd spend long weekends with me, gingerly trying to sit on my lap while I watched ballgames on TV.

"This lap taken?" he'd ask.

"Yes," I'd say.

"I'll just be a couple of hours," he'd claim, then step gently from the couch to my chair and curl up on my legs.

We were the oddest of couples: Him, slender and young; Me, mighty and middle-aged. He wore his hair short. Mine fell over the ears. He had a head like an ax. Mine was rounder, more like a throw pillow.

We'd take long and fitful walks along the boulevard, the dog and I. He'd pull. I'd snap the leash. He'd pull some more. I'd curse his ancestry and pull right back.

I am not the most powerful of men. I have Stockard Channing's shoulders and Woody Allen's hips. When opening the fridge, I sometimes require two good tugs. I'll use a 5-iron when a 7 would probably do. You get the idea: Don't mess with me ever.

"Easy," I'd say with a sharp tug, then, "EASY!!!" pulling on the leash with both arms.

"I just need to be patient and persistent," the beagle would tell himself. "Soon I'll have him trained."

Three times a day I would walk him like this. I found three to be the minimum number of walks required to keep him from piddling on my moccasins or spritzing the couch.

As owners do, we adjusted our lives to accommodate the new dog's personality quirks. We'd put the diaper pail on the table so the puppy couldn't steal them. Diapers are an excellent source of fiber, apparently, but the plastic doesn't digest well. We also learned to slide sideways through the front door when entering or leaving, to keep the puppy from dashing out and escaping, which usually resulted in a 30-minute chase involving three cars, 12 people, and a helicopter.

In a short time, the puppy became not only an annoyance but a cold-blooded killer.

It happened on a rainy Saturday, I think, when we had the kids' pet bunny, Lola, in the garage instead of the hut out back where she usually stayed. Most bunnies are waterproof, but apparently Lola was not.

"I'm bringing the bunny in," my wife would say every time the winter rains threatened.

"She's probably fine outside," I'd say.

"I'm bringing him in," my wife insisted.

As you can see, my wife was constantly getting her bunny pronouns mixed up, calling her a he, which would've been more damaging, except the bunny's name was Lola. L-O-L-A, Lola. Even 30 years ago, the Kinks might've been on to something.

In any case, the bunny was in the garage, in a little dog crate we used on airline flights, when the puppy escaped out the kitchen door and bounded innocently toward the cage, probably stopping a little too late—extending his front legs in a braking stance at the very last second on the slippery concrete, the way puppies and ponies do—and smacking nose first into the cage of the bunny, who took one look at the asinine creature that had just hurled itself at her cage and promptly fell over dead.

In the puppy's defense, dwarf bunnies have notoriously tiny hearts and can drop over dead at the slightest surprise or disappointment—an unkind remark or a tiny sip of box wine. The beagle had killed poor Lola with sheer, innocent puppy enthusiasm, like some smiley summer intern you dread seeing coming at you in the hallway.

"Honey?"

"Huh?"

"Lola's gone," my wife told me hours later.

"She escaped?"

"No, the puppy scared him to death," she explained, then told the story of how the little beagle got into the garage. Somehow, in the retelling of it, the murder became all my fault, though I'm not sure how. I'm pretty sure I was at a local diner eating hash browns at the time of the crime. Like most men, I never forget a good plate of potatoes.

"You'll bury him out back?" my wife asked.

"I was thinking cryogenics," I said.

"I think out back will be fine," she said.

Eulogies were said—"Dear Lola, have a good afterlife. We'll miss you sooooooo much"—which made it sound like the little bunny had merely gone off to summer camp rather than bunny heaven. It had been 3 years since the kids had actually fed her, their mother taking over the care of the bunny in their neglect. So tears were few, and the kids were able to return quickly to their other responsibilities—constantly e-mailing friends and going to every awful movie that comes out.

After two days of putting it off, I finally buried the bunny on a rainy afternoon, the cold January raindrops trickling down the back of my neck as I sought a proper burial site. It was like the grim scenes you see of Arlington National Cemetery on raw December days. There was sadness, and there was fog.

Should I put her in the tomato patch? No. How about over along the side of the house? Well, okay.

I started to dig but immediately hit several big rocks and then the soft cigar box casket of a tree fog we'd buried several months earlier. Mud was everywhere.

Note that it's time to move when you run out of pet burial space. The ghosts of a hundred hamsters, gold fish, lizards, and lady bugs hang over our little house. Their souls, I assume, off to a better spot. Someplace with bigger bathrooms and more closet space, I hope.

The rain was coming down harder now, and I realized this burial site wouldn't work. It was full up. No vacancy. So I looked left. I looked right. I flung the bunny bag in a neighbor's light-blue trash can, the safest, most-respectful place I could find under difficult circumstances. In many ways, it was akin to burial at sea.

"You did what?" co-workers said the next day when I explained how it happened.

"It was pouring," I explained.

"Did you tell your wife?"

"Of course not."

"I can't believe you did that," someone else said, like I was the killer and not merely the mortician.

"Look, I'm not defending it," I said.

"I'll never think of you the same way again," the co-worker said.

Which could only be an improvement. But hey, I never said I was St. Francis of Assisi. I have my weak moments, my ethical lapses, my small and very precious vices.

But, when the time comes, I will grant you this: If it is raining, or even threatening, I give my heirs complete permission to dispose of me in much the same manner. Or cremate me and sprinkle my ashes in my buddy Brian's backyard. He has a terrific place, and I always wanted to spend more time there. Back behind the spa, where the leaf blowers can't get me.

In the meantime, I have a murderer in my bed, still making those coffee sounds and still trying to figure out which end is heads and which end is tails. He's a granddog, actually. A loyal and tragic friend.

6

THE ROUGHHOUSING
HALL OF FAME

LITTLE KIDS aren't so tough. I find that if you slide a hand under their armpit and around their neck, you can flip 'em like a pork chop.

With this move, I have yet to find a 4-year-old I couldn't dominate in a living room roughhousing match. Some are stronger than I am. Most are quicker and meaner. Yet, my record is an impressive 1,400 victories, 0 losses, 2 ties.

In addition to that move I just described, I attribute my successful roughhousing career to superior conditioning. Most 4-year-olds just aren't in that great shape. When you drop down a class, to roughhouse with 2- or 3-year-olds, the field is even weaker. They train, most of them, with a steady diet of grape juice and Oreo cookies.

Some dads prefer roughhousing with older kids, but I find that too competitive and exhausting. An 8-year-old, pumped full of Pepsi, is a strong and worthy opponent. Should his bony knee collide with your fleshy thigh, it could leave a bruise. They also get revved up and—like orangutans—are prone to biting. So I concentrate on the 4-and-unders.

"What's your secret?" my friends are always asking.

"Hard work and conditioning," I explain. "And I never skip dessert."

Clearly, fatherhood is not for wimps.

The International Federation of Roughhousing has some clear and specific guidelines.

- No match should last longer than 45 minutes.
- Bloody noses should not be wiped on the new couch.
- If you knock something over, say a lamp or a chair, you must pick it up before Mom sees.

Other than that, the federation leaves most issues up to individual contestants. Scoring, for example, is very flexible. Say, for instance, you're laughing so hard that you spit up a little? That's 2 points for your opponent. Chip a tooth on the coffee table? Two points for you. The first half ends when everyone is sweaty and gasping for air and eyeing each other like wolves.

"Hey Dad."

"Hey what?"

"Hey *this*!" the kid will say, throw a pillow in your face and pounce on your shoulder. With that, the second half begins.

Any dad considering taking up competitive roughhousing should follow a few simple guidelines. First, make sure all of your opponents have used the bathroom. There have been several examples where giggle-fits led to accidents. Good bladder control is paramount, for kids as well as fathers.

Once the match begins, your first goal is to gauge your opponent's strength. With a 4-year-old, a full body slam will not take much more effort than say, opening a letter from your alumni association. Don't let that discourage you. For it's important to show him who the boss is right away.

The next step is to measure his quickness. A 4-year-old is alarmingly quick. He will spin, roll, pivot, pirouette, unravel, somersault, shiver, shake, alligator, cough, crow hop, sputter, boogie, spit, and twist. Some will even squeeze themselves into little piles of puss. Don't be fooled by this.

Instead, use your superior strength and body weight to maintain control and crush their spirit.

"I am the King of all Kids!" I often yell during matches.

"Yeah? Prove it!" they will yell back.

"Okay, just don't hurt me," I answer, and more violence ensues.

Occasionally, someone will get a little hurt and call time-out. Under international rules, time-outs are unlimited. But beware of injury time-outs. It is customary, particularly among 6-year-olds, to call an injury timeout when behind in a match, then use the time-out to regain position.

Though this cannot be stopped, you don't want to be taken by surprise. Just grab the little cheater's legs and pile drive him into the couch.

Daughters are as adept at roughhousing as sons, but they are prone to more giggling and won't attempt to kill you when you're not looking. Boys, on the other hand, not fully realizing the limits of a living room roughhousing match and answering some inner Oedipal need, may attempt to decapitate you with a fireplace tool. My advice? With boys, never turn your back.

Speaking of young Oedipus, one note about mothers: Mothers are notoriously opposed to roughhousing of any kind. At best they will tolerate it. At worst, they will ban it from the house and cut you, the dad, off from sex for a month.

My guess is that they are envious of the bonds you are forming with your children. A mother can clean a house for 40 years and no one will pause to say thanks. But roughhouse with a kid for 30 minutes, and he'll nominate you for Dad of the Year. It's just one reason why roughhousing is quickly becoming our national pastime.

So every once in a while, I recommend grabbing the wife from behind, pinning her down, and giving her a good noogie on the top of her pretty head. It's worth 4 points, and not only does this include them in the game, it also reinforces who is boss around your house.

It's you, right?

Yeah, right.

7

ADVENTURES IN BABYSITTING

I HAVE ORDERED, without even realizing it at first, what is known in the movie business as Combo No. 3: medium popcorn plus medium Coke. The popcorn comes in a bag. The Coke comes in a giant vat that should include a catheter. For if you drink this entire thing, there is no way you won't be spending half the movie in the restroom.

"Butter?" the snack counter clerk asks.

"Of course," I say.

Had I ordered the medium popcorn and medium Coke individually, it would've cost me $10. But since it's one of the snack bar's combo items (the No. 3), it only costs me. . . . wait, 10 bucks?

I don't bother to inquire. I'm too busy marveling over the fact that the soda dispenser is a good 15 steps away from the cash register and popcorn. If the medium drink comes in a vat, what sort of container would be required for a large drink? A swimming pool? And how the hell do they get that back and forth?

"Will that be all?" the clerk asks.

"Isn't that enough?" I say.

"Ten dollars," he says.

Magical Saturday evenings out with friends don't just happen. They are the product of heavy-duty planning. Phone calls that began on Wednesday, probably 10 of them in all. "You guys free?" "Let me check." It's the back and forth of two couples cross-checking their busy calendars, lining up sitters, finding a movie no one has seen yet. That sort of thing.

"Saturday?" the little girl asks.

"Just for a couple hours," her mother says.

"Saturday I was working on my project," the little girl whines.

The little girl is wonderful in a hundred wonderful ways but babysitting isn't really one of them. She is smart. Reliable. Resourceful. Ceaselessly charming. In her mind, such qualities shouldn't be wasted on younger siblings.

"Saturday?" she asks again, as if chewing on the same piece of meat.

The little girl is in junior high now, plenty old enough to watch her toddler brother for a couple of hours on a Saturday night, when she wouldn't be working on her project anyway. Instead, she would be e-mailing all her little friends to confirm that they weren't doing anything exciting either. Such information is vital to an eighth-grader's mental well-being. Once she was done with that, she'd read one of those teen magazines she is so fond of now.

"How to Get the Best Butt Possible!" screams the headline on the cover. Or *"Which Hot Celebrity Do You Resemble Most?"* There are horoscopes as well.

Since our lovely and patient older daughter left for college, we have had mixed results with sitters. Our older daughter was a reliable and willing sitter for us, able to trade her services as a sitter for new clothes and tanks of gas for her Civic. Some kids can barter, and some kids can't. Well, actually, they can all barter, some are just better at it. And the older daughter was the barter champ.

She made a fortune sitting for other families as well, bringing home $70–$80 for a five-hour shift. I wondered, as she came in the door clicking off 20s, whether she had also painted the kitchen and re-glazed some windows. But she said no, it was strictly for babysitting the anguished children of earnest parents.

"These moms, they pay a lot," she explained.

"Evidently," I said.

"Sometimes, I make a hundred," she said.

"Just for sitting?" I said.

When I heard "a hundred," I was considering taking some babysitting gigs myself. One-hundred dollars, tax free? How often do I get to have 100 bucks in my pocket. Usually, I'm relegated to handing out 20s like some sort of human ATM: haircuts, birthday gifts, gas. As a dad, I'm a dispenser, not a collector. I've thought seriously of having an ATM slot installed in my forehead. I have the room for it. They could simply push my nose and 20s would cascade out.

But these babysitting opportunities could change everything. If I could pick up one or two gigs a week, I might be able to sock a little money away. One day, I might be able to afford that Volvo SUV I've been eyeing.

"Dad?"

"Huh?"

"I'm sick."

That's how I got my first gig. It was several years ago. The lovely and patient older daughter was sitting for the Brooks girls. It was a good job to watch the Brooks girls. First, they were girls, which cut down on the felonies and assaults you'd experience babysitting boys of a comparable age. Second, Jeff has this big house up the hill, the kind you're always dreaming about. The kitchen alone is the size of Terminal 4 at LAX. Tile everywhere.

"I think I'm going to throw up," the older daughter moaned over the phone.

It was a Friday night, and I'd just gotten home from work. No one else was around. They left no notes. Or food, for that matter. I was looking forward to nesting in front of the TV with a cold frosty beverage and cheering the Laker Girls.

Instead, there was my sick daughter on the phone, up at the Brooks house, about to throw up all over their Ethan Allen sofa. I paused and thought.

"Okay, I'll be right up," I finally told her.

When I walked in, the Lakers were on Jeff's big-screen TV. I don't know what Jeff sells, but he sells a lot of it. Even after he and his wife leave for an evening out, there are still three cars in the circular driveway.

"You okay?" I asked.

"I think I have a fever," said my daughter.

I knew just what to do. I got her a wash cloth and a bucket. The Lakers were rallying. This wouldn't be so bad. The kids were all asleep by now anyway.

Then my wife swung by later to pick up our sick daughter, leaving me in charge. I checked the fridge. I sat back down and put my feet up on the coffee table. Nope, this wouldn't be so bad at all.

I fretted only once. Okay, twice. First, I fretted over the thought that one of the kids would come downstairs to find me, a virtual stranger, with his feet up on the coffee table and drinking her daddy's beer—the good kind, not the sale stuff I buy at home. She would run screaming back upstairs to her three sisters, and they would return in force, tie me up, beat me silly with their Princess Diaries books (the pink hard covers). Considering how smart and aggressive girls are today, their reading habits could use a little work.

"Please, couldn't you hit me with something better?" I'd plead.

"Meg Cabot rules!" they'd scream, hurting me more with those words than any physical abuse ever could.

I fretted too, that Jeff and his wife, a willowy redhead, would return home and find me in the house and think something tragic had happened, when really all that had happened was that I had consumed two of his premium beers and finished those Cape Cod potato chips I can't get enough of. I feared that Jeff and Helen would think the worst, Helen would pass out, and there I'd be, a babysitter without a tip.

Turns out, none of that happened. The kids slept straight through, and Jeff and Helen returned home without incident—Helen looking especially great in heels. I turned down money, though I wish Jeff had insisted just a bit more. Maybe it was the way I had my feet up on the coffee table when they walked in the door. I was half-asleep, with a can of Pringles in my lap, reading one of Helen's fashion magazines. "Why Men Leave" was the article, I think. They never really told you why.

But I digress. For we are out ourselves this Saturday night, with Steve and Susan, two new friends who still appreciate our company. We have purchased vast quantities of popcorn and soda. Most of our older friends seem completely dispassionate about us lately. So we are auditioning new friends. Steve and Susan seem awfully promising.

"Let's go," I tell Steve, and we head into the theater.

We had sent the wives in earlier to find some seats, always a gamble. In this case, they took seats in the middle of the row, 15 chairs on either side. Men like aisle seats. If you take one thing away from this book, it should be that men prefer aisle seats.

"Nice seats," I lie.

"Way to go, girls," lies Steve.

We trip over 15 sets of ankles to get to our seats, while trying not to spill the popcorn or the soft drinks. But they are fine seats, smack dab in the middle of the theater. We settle in with our snacks and check out the previews. I am not normally a funny guy—frankly, I find humor a crutch—except for the 5 minutes before a movie begins. I can riff on trailers, joke about the commercials. In the 5 minutes before a movie starts, I'm Billy Crystal reborn.

After a preview of a grim movie about a woman who loses her daughter on a big jetliner, I say pretty loud, "Could've been worse. She coulda lost her laptop," and 10 people around us laugh.

See, funny stuff like that just pours out of me. I think it might have something to do with that goofy, butterlike chemical they put on popcorn.

As the trailers play, the seats fill in. Eventually, the guy with the anvil head who always sits in front of me at concerts and ball games takes his place. He has a crew cut, but that doesn't matter. His head is so huge on its own that he doesn't need hair. He blocks my view of the screen without it. His head reminds me of those fake boulders they put out in center field at Angel Stadium. I'm sure he is nice man. He just happens to have a really, really humongous head.

Then Slurpee Man arrives and sits directly to my right. You may have been exposed to Slurpee Man. He gets the 32-ounce Slurpee and proceeds to suck the icy drink noisily through the straw the entire movie. Frankly, I don't think he just sucks. I think he blows as well. First, he sucks a little in, then he sends it back through the straw in a sort of Slurpee loop. That way, he won't run out of Slurpee. He is recycling it so that it will last the entire movie. I'm sure he is a nice man as well.

Slurpee Man quickly takes command of our mutual arm rest. Legally, since I was here first, I should get dibs on the arm rest. It's in the multiplex code of conduct. Newcomers do not get the armrest. In response, I take over my wife's armrest.

"What are you doing?" she asks.

"Seizing your armrest," I say.

"I was here first," she says, like that means anything anymore.

Up on the screen, the trailers are ending. They flash the standard warning about turning off cell phones and pagers as a courtesy to those around you. I'm all for courtesy. It's such an afterthought these days.

"That's directed right at you," I whisper to my wife when the cell phone warning flashes on the screen.

She swears that she has turned off the cell phone, but invariably in the second act of any movie her cell phone rings, during one of the quiet moments when all you can hear otherwise is the click-click-click of the projector and the lip/saliva sounds of an important on-screen kiss.

Last movie, it happened and she spent 3 minutes talking to whoever it was, probably one of our daughters, whose almost every conversation is done by cell phone. If they ever have to speak face-to-face, my daughters wouldn't know what to do.

"Put it away, put it away," I kept saying, as people shushed us all around. It's a bad moment when you realize you can become, even momentarily, the sort of people you otherwise despise.

"Shussssssssssssh," said the guy with the anvil head, otherwise a very nice guy.

Now tonight, theater management seems ready for us. They have flashed this cell phone notice prominently, leaving the impression that anyone who violates the policy will be immediately beheaded. Fair enough, I say. We are reaching the point where a few public beheadings now and then would probably do society good.

"I apologize in advance over what will happen tonight," I tell Steve and Susan.

"I've turned it off," my wife promises.

"Whatever happens, I'm sorry," I say loud enough so every one around us can hear, even the guy with the anvil head in front of me. The last thing I need is for him to be shushing me again.

Sure enough, about an hour into the movie, I see my wife digging for her cell phone. A raspy sound, like a putty knife to wood, is coming from her purse. Sean Penn is up on the screen, trying his hardest to pretend he's taller than he really is. Nicole Kidman just looks down at him and smirks. It is a compelling moment.

"You what?" I hear my wife whisper into the cell phone.

"Click-click-click," says the projector.

"Just put some ice on it," my wife says.

"Slurp-slurp-slurp," goes Slurpee Man.

"Huh?" my wife asks.

"What's wrong?" I ask, now worried.

"Shuusssssh," says some clown behind us.

In hushed tones, my wife explains that the little girl was dishing out ice cream, when she licked the scoop. You know about licking the scoop. It's frowned upon, but nearly everybody does it. Somehow, ice cream tastes better right from the scoop. Fresher and more creamy.

But as she was enjoying the ice cream directly from the scoop, her tongue became stuck to the cold metal scoop. Evidently, the scoop is now stuck to her tongue, as she tries to tell her mother what happened over a cell phone in a quiet theater.

"You'll be all right," her mother assures her.

"Buth my tongth ith th-uck," our daughter explained, "toth da scoopah."

"Is everything all right?" Susan asked.

"Shhhhhh," said the people behind us.

"Click-click-click," went the projector.

Of course, everything was all right. With babysitters, the crisis is usually pretty minor, even if at the time it seems major. Our daughter's tongue was fine—she put ice on it, of all things—and we were able to finish out the movie, then return home for a glass of wine and a fuller explanation of the ice cream scoop incident. Before they left, Steve and Susan could not have been more gracious and insisted we should get together again soon, when I'm sure what they meant was "If we can't absolutely find anybody else."

In any event, we hope to go out again soon, my wife and I. We'll find a free night, line up a sitter. I checked our schedule. According to our calendar, the year 2019 looks very promising.

A Few of My Favorite Things

I HAVE A DIFFERENT spin on things than normal people do. I believe that bratwurst is God's most perfect food. That all babies are bonus babies. That pepper is far superior to salt.

That 6 in the morning is the best time of day. That all hours are happy hours.

You wouldn't believe some of the things I believe. That true love emanates from the liver, not the heart. It's why, when we get a little liquor in us, we're more amorous than ever. All our desires, all our cravings begin right there in the liver, refuge of our sweetest, most complex emotions.

But somehow, "heart" just sounds better. "I left my liver in San Francisco" just doesn't have the same drippy ring. Or how about Shakespeare? "But break my liver, for I must hold my tongue." Forget it.

Yes, I have a different spin. I believe that the airport is often the most memorable part of the trip. Not the best, just the most memorable. I believe that bacon is an aphrodisiac, that bears have more fun than people do, that eyeglasses make you smarter.

I believe that funeral homes always have the best-kept lawns in town (go figure). I believe that sports bars serve the best burgers.

I believe that when you're in a bad job, every day feels like Monday, that when you're in a great job, every day feels like Friday. And that most of us have jobs that feel like Tuesday through Thursday.

I believe that apples are superior to oranges, rib eyes are superior to fillets, and that Bonnie was superior to Clyde.

If asked, I can justify all these beliefs with the sort of half-baked arguments you hear in Congress or your local school board. I believe in half-baked arguments. I believe all meat should be medium rare and that brownies and arguments should be half-baked.

I believe we begin dying the day we stop having fun. I believe a dirty mind is a healthy mind or at least a normal mind, so we should quit being so rough on ourselves. I believe in risqué jokes and laughing till you cry.

I believe blizzards are superior to hurricanes, potatoes are superior to rice, and vodka is superior to gin.

I believe in butter on oatmeal and blueberries in pancakes. I believe horseradish is the best condiment and that it makes you live not only longer but better.

I believe rain on a windowpane is somehow soothing, and the best part of morning coffee is the way a warm ceramic cup feels against your hand.

I believe wood floors should creak and that old houses should rattle. I believe in paying a little more for a good computer.

I believe that good conversation is its own food group, and as necessary as vegetables and calcium to a healthy life. I believe good conversation invigorates, enlightens, and relaxes us. I wish you could buy it on the open market.

Instead, we have friends. I believe in friends, mostly. The good ones last a lifetime and what else can you say that about anymore. Nothing lasts a lifetime but a good buddy and property taxes.

I believe in the advantages of laughter, on a physical and emotional level. I believe in Groucho and Woody, Hawkeye, and Trapper John. In fact, I like to believe that Hawkeye Pierce returned from Korea and briefly dated Mary Richards.

I believe in the restorative powers of a good quip. In Jack Benny and Bob Newhart. In Bill Murray and George Carlin. A good quip frees us from our fears.

I believe in autumn days, tailgate parties, and the snap-hiss of a freshly opened beverage. I believe in throwing on first down. I believe in going for it on fourth and one.

I believe in rally caps and ninth-inning comebacks. In walk-off homeruns. In the suicide squeeze.

I believe in hot dogs, red onions, and iceberg lettuce. I believe all other lettuces are sad, droopy excuses for lettuce. I know this is controversial, but that's what I believe.

I believe in the written word. I believe in Keillor and Twain, Fitzgerald and Steinbeck. I believe in Roth and Updike. Edward Abbey. Tom Robbins. I believe most books are too long, including probably this one. I believe the best writing reveals our little truths and an endearing humanity.

I believe in yard work and raking and piles of maple leaves high as your head. I believe in wood smoke and apple cider. I believe in wool. That's right, wool.

I believe in long drives when you don't need to be anyplace at any special times. I believe in checking your own oil. I believe in early starts.

I believe in The Who and the Beatles, James Taylor and Miles Davis. I believe in bands with horn sections and Latin percussionists. I believe that if I had it to do all over again, I would've been a drummer.

I believe in live bait and rowboats without motors. I believe in bluegills and walleyed pike. I believe Nitschke was better than Butkus.

I believe in strong minds, healthy bodies, white bread, and 8-penny nails. I believe in WD-40 and titanium drill bits. Like many men, I believe that preparation is the key to good painting.

I believe in firm handshakes, rough hugs, and pats on the back. I believe air kisses aren't only insulting, they're vulgar. Under the right circumstances, I believe in a good slap on the ass.

I believe in old juke boxes, a Friday night game of pool, and blonde barmaids named Freddy. I believe in cheeseburgers at midnight and aspirin for breakfast. At least occasionally.

I believe in eggs at Easter, cigars at Halloween, and Bloody Marys on Mardi Gras morning. I believe in buying gifts on Christmas Eve. Sudden-death shopping. Overtime, baby.

I believe you get what you deserve, you reap what you sow, you get what you pay for.

I believe in love. The American flag. Valor and humility. Quiet heroes and courage. Pat Tillman and his teammates in green.

And, finally, I believe in perseverance. In fact, I may believe in perseverance more than I believe in anything else. Except heart, of course. Heart is nearly everything.

Not to be confused, of course, with the liver. The liver is where it all starts—the symbol of all that is best in us.

9

THE HOUSE OF HICCUPS

LATELY, WE'VE all been having dinner together again, an absolute aberration in these times of fractured families and fast-paced lives. According to the experts, families rarely sit down for dinner together anymore. So praise the lord and pass the mashed potatoes.

"This is good, Mom," the boy says.

"You're on a roll," says the older daughter.

"Thank you," says their mother, who has been making them great meals now for almost 20 years. Nice of them to notice this. Guess she's on a roll.

"I learned a new word today," I say. "Want to hear it?"

One of them grunts. At least I think it was a grunt. It might've been one of those unintentional bodily sounds that they never seem to hear themselves emit. Being an optimist, I assume it was a grunt.

"Sure, Dad," one of them says.

"Pass the butter," says another.

"Sit up straight," says their mother.

I tell them the word. Canthus. It's the angle formed where the lids join on either side of the eye. On the outside, where brow and cheekbone meet. On the inside, the vale of tears. Canthus. It's an interesting, underused word for a lovely, banked curve in the human face.

"I thought you could use it in Scrabble," I say.

"That's a good one, Dad."

"Yeah, Dad," someone says. "Good one."

Someone else grunts. At least I think it's a grunt.

"Please pass the corn," says my wife.

Some families are obsessed with money. Some families are obsessed with power. Our family is obsessed with pork chops and chopped salads.

Food is our passion. At breakfast, we'll talk about lunch. At Thanksgiving dinner, we'll talk about what we'll have at Christmas.

"Please pass the salad dressing," says the little girl.

I'm a big believer in buffet-style eating. You leave the serving dishes on the counter, and everybody helps themselves. My wife prefers to have the dishes on the table, where we must pass them to each other on demand. She believes this teaches the children teamwork and good manners. It is one of the fundamental issues that divide our marriage.

Because here's what happens. Inevitably, someone will ask for more mashed potatoes. "Can you please pass the mashed potatoes?" that person will say. The person nearest the mashed potatoes will begin to pass the dish, and then she'll realize she really needs more potatoes herself and will scoop pretty much all of the remaining mashed potatoes from the serving dish onto her own plate before passing the dish. This produces roughly the same blast of sound you hear when someone drops a cherry bomb down a grade school commode.

"MOMMMMMMMM!"

"What?"

"He took all the mashed potatoes!"

"There's more mashed potatoes in the kitchen," their mother explains calmly.

"But Mom . . . !"

"Just get more mashed potatoes," she urges.

At which point someone gets the hiccups. At our dinners, at least one person always gets the hiccups. It's a family tradition, like red hair and bad backswings.

"Hiccccccc!" someone gasps.

The table explodes with laughter.

"Hiiiiiiiccccccc!"

I don't know about your hiccups, but ours start down around our toes and work their way up the body. They hiccup the way Mickey Mantle swung, with every muscle, saving nothing for thee later innings.

Our hiccups also get progressively louder. And there is no "up" in our hiccups, only the hic part. If you waited around for the "up," you'd be waiting a very long time.

"Hiiiiiicccc!"

"Just excuse yourself from the table," their mother advises.

"Hiiiiiiiiiiiiiiiiiiiiiiiiiiiiiiiiic!"

"Now!" she says.

At this point, the others are laughing into their pork chops. Some have their hands over their faces and are turning red. Others have turned sideways in their chairs and are doubled over as if their appendix is about to burst. Since this happens nearly every night, you'd think it would get old. Not so far.

"I've only had the hiccups twice in my life," their mother explains.

"Really, Mom?" the little girl asks.

They treat this confession the same way you would if someone said they've never seen a snowflake or a rainbow. It is unbelievable to them that someone could go 45 years and get hiccups only twice. Almost a medical miracle.

Unlike the rest of us, my wife obviously doesn't wolf down her food. She chews every bite; she savors the flavors and the marinades, the careful blend of spices she worked so hard to get right.

The others, meanwhile, load food into their mouths as if over-stuffing a clothes washer, and then they chase it with some milk and a biscuit if one's handy. They chew once—twice on a good day—then swallow the food mostly whole, where it proceeds down their esophagus and—stop me if I'm getting too technical—clogs their hiccup pipe. In our family, the hiccup pipe is about 4 inches in diameter, a little near the heart. Once it gets clogged, it takes about half an hour to flush itself.

"Hiiiiiiiiiiiiiiiicc!" says the little girl.

More and more, our family dinners resemble P.E. class at a clown college. The little girl says that when she eats dinner at other people's homes, the meals can be quite serious as the father pontificates on OPEC prices or what's been going on in The Hague. I tried that once. They laughed me right off the stage.

"The Rhymers have fun dinners, too," the little girl explains. "Mr. Rhymer is sooooooo funny."

The implication being that I am not, of course. But then, I don't need to be. I am surrounded by comedians with clogged hiccup pipes.

"Mr. Rhymer . . . he's a comedy writer," the little girl says.

"He is?" says the boy.

"He is?" I say.

I always wondered why Mr. Rhymer never went to work. He just seems to sit around all day in his bath robe, walking the dog, watching airplanes. He starts his annual Christmas letter in, like, July.

"You should be a comedy writer, Dad," someone says.

"Good idea," I say.

Tonight, it is the little girl's turn to get the hiccups. As the others laugh, she excuses herself from the table. The further she gets from the table, the louder her hiccups get. If she were, theoretically, to get on a plane bound for Cleveland, you could still hear her hiccuping over Omaha.

"Stand on you head," her brother urges.

"Hold your breath," says the older daughter.

"Hiiiiiiiiiic," says the little girl, tears of laughter filling her eyes.

Fortunately, no one has suggested getting a glass of water, which someone almost always does. This results in the sort of spit-takes you used to see on Carson, when Dom DeLuise was a guest. The next thing you know, I'm repainting the kitchen.

"Drink some water," says her brother.

"Wait!" I say.

"What?"

"Hold off on the water," I say.

"Oh Dad . . ."

"You should see her drink water, Dad," says the boy.

"It comes right out her nose," says the older daughter.

"Maybe next time," I promise.

At the far end of the table, the toddler. He is the worst sort of subversive—quiet and contemplative—40 pounds of trouble in a 20-pound can. He takes advantage of his siblings' hiccup outbreaks to stealthily slip peas and carrots to the dogs waiting beneath his chair. Without him, our pets would hardly get any vegetables at all. He is marvelously coy about it, dropping them individually, so that the dogs don't eat too quickly and get the hiccups, too.

Even at 2, the baby realizes that there's only so many hiccups one house can take. He reflects back to dinners in the womb, which were much more civil than anything he has experienced here. He used to get hiccups back then, but they weren't debilitating, as they seem to be with these people.

"Hiiiiiiiic," says the little girl.

"Go lie down," says her mother.

After dinner, the hiccup victim gets some of the finest medical treatment available in America. Inevitably, one person will place a pillow under their feet and try to stuff a dirty sock into the hiccup victim's mouth. I remember it as the same treatment you used to get in the dorm when you had the flu. It makes me nostalgic for the good old days.

"I really like these family dinners," I tell my wife.

"It's nice," she says, "that we can be together like this."

"Anybody want pie?" barks the boy.

"We have pie?" I say.

"No," he says. "I was just wondering if anybody wanted some."

"If we had it," I say.

"Exactly," says the boy.

"That makes sense," I tell his mother.

"I'll have pie," says the older daughter.

More than the others, the boy needs his nourishment. You know how teenagers are. This morning, he woke up 6 inches taller than when he went to bed last night. Since lunch alone, he has grown 4 inches. He is like a 4-H livestock project we can never unload. By next week, he may no longer be able to fit inside the house.

"I sure could use some pie," he says.

Dessert is a special time for us. We eat ice cream and sweets like a Mormon family does, in great gobs on the sort of big platters usually reserved for slabs of meat at Easter. It's a tribute to our Irish metabolism that we don't all weigh, say, 6,000 pounds apiece. Wisecracks must burn a lot of calories.

"I'll make brownies," says the boy.

"I love brownies," says his big sister.

"Hiiiiiic," says the little girl, which now substitutes for the phrase "Yes, I'd like some" in our family.

They like their brownies medium rare, soft and chewy in the middle, the way you'd cook a nice piece of sirloin. I explain to them that brownies have eggs in them and that eggs can be dangerous unless heated properly.

"Not these brownies, Dad," says the little girl.

"These brownies don't have eggs," says her mother.

I can't imagine how you can have any baked product without eggs. But more and more, the world surprises me. Just when I think I have seen it all, along comes an egg-free batch of brownies.

"Wow," I say, the way I did the very first time I saw an X-ray of my own teeth.

In the hands of experts like these, a brownie is without a doubt our finest dessert. In fact, I'm willing to bet that if you put out a table of great desserts—cherry pie, chocolate cake, Jell-O—the brownies would be the first to go. That's just my hunch, but I feel very certain about it.

"You want two, Dad?" they say when the brownies are done.

"Sure, if you're being skimpy," I say.

"Give Dad three," one of them whispers.

Hey, remember, these brownies don't have eggs. I could eat a dozen of them, and I would only get stronger, more powerful. People are always asking me: "How can one man be so darned strong? So powerful? Yet so sickly?"

"Brownies," I answer. The more the merrier. And a big tall glass of milk.

Hicccccc!

10

AN EXPERIMENT IN
COMMUNAL LIVING

I WANT TO START a commune, but I am reminded by my wife that we can't even camp happily together within our own family, that a little hardship seems to bring out the worst in us. There is, after all, a tent, camping stove, and other gear tucked safely out of the way in the corner of the garage, rarely used. A $500 jungle gym for moths and spiders.

When we camped—three entire times—it was in grand fashion. I rented a big tent and bought sleeping bags and heaps of firewood. I purchased hot dogs and marshmallows, soft drinks and buns. We were the anti-Donner Party. If we perished in the mountains, it would be from the strain of lifting cases of cream soda from the trunk.

"I love camping," the lovely and patient older daughter said, even though we hadn't left the driveway. What appealed to her, I think, was buying lots of new things then cramming it all into the back of the minivan. As a teenager, she was turned on by the mere sight of so many credit card receipts.

"Have a good time," my wife said.

"Wait, you're not coming?"

"Have a great time," she repeated.

My wife comes from a family that has never left the pavement. Indoor people, they run from the house to the car as if a meteor might catch them on the chin. When they arrive at their destination, usually some mall or Indian casino, they dash inside. Part of it is the inclement Florida weather they are often forced to deal with. In January, morning temperatures can dip well into the 60s.

"Do you have matches?" my wife asked.

"Matches?"

"You know, to start the fire," she said.

"Fire?"

Of course, I never did much camping either. My family's idea of roughing it was staying at the Holiday Inn instead of the Hilton. We never went anywhere that didn't have an ice machine 10 steps down the hall.

"Go get me some ice," were the first words my father always barked after we'd dragged our luggage to the hotel room.

So we did.

But here my wife and I were in California, home to some of the nation's best camping. Besides, too much central air-conditioning leaves the legs and arms feeling like chilled meat. I'd grab the boy playfully, and it'd be like lifting cold rib eyes from the fridge. By August, we were ready to actually go outside.

"Did we bring cards?" the older daughter asked.

"I've got my Visa," I said.

"I meant playing cards, Dad."

"What about a TV?" asked the boy, suddenly concerned.

The boy, then 10, wasn't yet aware that nature hadn't been wired for cable. It will be one day, but not yet.

In fact, he would soon learn that much of nature didn't even have hot tubs or towels. Boy, was the boy ever in for a surprise.

"There'll be plenty of TVs," I lied, eager to get them in the car.

And into the car we went, the two girls and the boy, off into the mountains behind Pasadena. As soon as we passed the last Jack in the Box, we knew it was time to stop.

"How about here?" I said.

"This looks great," said the little girl.

Here's why I love camping:

- The phone never rings.
- The doorbell doesn't buzz.
- There are no visible clocks.
- No remotes, pagers, or Blackberries.
- The gardeners' Weed Eaters don't wake me.

- My kids' strange little friends aren't constantly wandering through my line of vision.
- The microwave isn't always beep-beep-beeping.
- There is no stack of unpaid bills looming on the desk.
- Essentially, there are no neighbors.
- At night, the crickets.
- At night, the stars.
- A cracking fire makes you forget deadlines, bosses, and petty obligations.
- You can sleep in your clothes, like a vagrant.

There are a hundred other things I love about camping. I love the way hot dogs taste after you cook them on a stick. I love the way faces look in firelight. I love the ghost stories. And the sound of a cooler lid opening and the beer-hiss that follows.

I could camp six or eight times a year and never get bored with it. There are so many fine camp sites around California, in the mountains and by the sea. Some need to be reserved far in advance, but some very good ones allow you to just show up.

My son and I, camping together when he was 12, will never forget the sound of a Dodger game on the radio, 100 miles away, as the fire began to die and the marshmallows turned black as a boot.

Our few experiences camping were so pleasant—so occasionally profound—that I went out and invested in hundreds of dollars worth of tents, lanterns, pancake pans, and bug repellant.

We've used them once. Part of it is that our weekends are over-packed with youth sports, dances, and school fairs. The other part, I realized far too late, is that our kids are like their grandparents: They really don't like the dirt. After a day or two of camping, they would get cranky and their moods would descend from there. A family that rarely fights would get into arguments that resembled the third act of Wagner's "Gotterdammerung," fiery and war like.

Still, I've got this urge to start a commune.

I suggest approaching our very best friends about this, "best" being a relative term. Among all our friends, the best ones are the ones we are most comfortable with. It implies neither rank nor quality, though they are some of the finest friends we've ever had.

"You don't even like going to dinner with them," my wife notes.

"I just hate hearing all about their kids going to Yale," I tell her.

"Then how," she asks, "are you going to tolerate them all the time?"

By being selective, that's how. In soccer and softball, success depends on how well you draft your team. Communes shouldn't be any different. In fact, chances are we'll be the first commune to feature a Team Mom.

I'd start the commune by recruiting handsome, well-behaved pets, for I have always believed that a bad pet can destroy a home's ambience worse that a drunken uncle or a surly teen. Drunken uncles, for the most part, don't gnaw on my dress shoes, and most won't urinate on the rugs.

In our commune, we'd prefer the almost hairless smaller breeds. They fit best on my lap and don't leave piles of fur under the tables and in the couches, where it will eventually wind up in my salads and my sheets. Nothing's worse than awaking from one of my fever dreams and gagging on some clump of cocker spaniel hair. From what I've been able to observe, pet hair is one of the few natural resources that is actually on the increase.

Then I'd interview the kids. I'd insist on children who look you straight in the eye and speak when spoken to. I don't know if there are any such kids left, but that's my template. They would have to appreciate Emerson, Lake & Palmer and Steinbeck and old Bob Newhart albums. They'd have to know a little history. For example, when the great quarterbacks are mentioned, they'd bring up Bart Starr's name and, of course, Staubach. When discussing shortstops, they'd never leave out Don Kessinger.

The dads would have to have equal intellectual range, plus the ability to make me laugh. I look for one thing in my male friends and that is a wry outlook toward life and the tendency to make a joke out of nearly everything they encounter. To me, a flip remark in just the right circumstances is better than a backrub, better than a good Beaujolais, the equal of sex. Indeed, I remember flip remarks far longer than I remember most sessions of lovemaking, which, you'll have to admit, become a bit of a blur after age 26 or so.

Then I'd interview the women of my commune. First, I'd pick my wife since she's used to me and I'm used to her and I still like the way she looks in a sweater. I still appreciate and marvel over her observations about life and her judgments about people and the way she handles the children. What more could you ask from a mate? If she'd just quit nagging me about the garage, she'd almost be perfect.

Then I'd give Nancy a free pass. Nancy is Bill's wife, and she stopped aging at about 32. Seriously, it's as if the aging process just shut down. Her teeth sparkle, and she always giggles politely at my little jokes while our two families lounge around the beach on long summer days, talking about some article we read in *Newsweek*. Nancy looks like we suspected sorority girls would look later in life but seldom do. She's a first draft pick in any commune.

Then I'd pick Debbie, my wife's very funny friend. It's hard to describe Debbie except to say that when you're standing around the kitchen swilling Chardonnay and waiting for someone to toss the salad, Debbie can say the funniest, most outlandish things. Like all good humor, her observations are character-based and dead-on true. I'd compare her to Cosby, except she's shorter, whiter, and makes better jalapeño cornbread.

It would start as a small commune. On Monday, we'd all watch *Monday Night Football* together. Tuesday would be bingo night and Wednesday would be reserved for poker and cigars. Thursday would be a reading night, and Friday night we'd all stay up late together watching movies.

I don't know what we'd do the other nights. I certainly wouldn't mind just sitting around talking one night, like we used to in the freshman dorm, which by the way is the model for this commune. I've always believed that the free flow of idiotic ideas is the lifeblood of any family, large or small.

Commune rules would be few, except that we could add members only with unanimous votes. We could drop members by unanimous votes as well, except for me, the eccentric founding father of this commune.

As it states in the bylaws, stolen from a local condo association: "No one shall kick out the founding father. He has his faults, sure, but without him there'd be no commune and we'd all be stuck back in our boring little lives, sneaking out once a week maybe to eat at the Red Lobster or catch some lousy Jennifer Lopez movie. Our founding father deserves better than that, for he is a true visionary and almost Lincolnesque in his leadership."

Or something like that. The exact wording isn't import. The point is that communes are about to make a comeback. And our little family—an odd mix of naturalists, pacifists, animists, Republicans, and pro wrestling fans—has never been more ready.

"Dad wants to start a *what*?" the older daughter asks when she gets wind of our changing lifestyle.

"He wants to start a commune."

"Like Manson?"

"More like Thoreau," I say.

"Who's Thoreau?" the little girl asks.

We'll also have a study night.

11

JACK DANIEL'S MAKES MUSTARD

Dear Dad,

How are things up there in the skyboxes? I thought I'd catch you up on a few things you might've missed down here while you were up there practicing chip shots with Snead and Hogan. I just gotta ask: In Heaven, do you chip in every time?

Things are great down here, and I'm not being cliché when I say "wish you were here." There's a lot going on, and I miss your observations on the day-to-day triumphs and idiocies of modern man. Have I mentioned that Jack Daniel's now makes mustard? Believe me, that's only the beginning.

In the decade you've been gone, a lot has happened, both good and bad. Yes, Jack Daniel's makes mustard (good) and the best movies coming out of Hollywood are cartoons (bad), though as cartoons go, they're a far cry from Bugs Bunny. Let me just say, I have had to watch *Shreck 2* about 50 times in the past week and admire it more with each successive viewing. I get up mornings with your youngest grandkid, the one who looks like Sonny Jurgensen, and we pretzel our legs over each other and watch *Shreck 2* while the rest of the family sleeps. It's a lot better than it sounds, believe me. Sometimes we eat Cheerios together right out of the box.

Let's see, what else is new? The job at the paper is going okay. Let me just say that the workplace has changed since you retired 15 years ago. No drinking at lunch. No kissing in the supply closet. You're lucky if you can find a colleague who'll cuss a little or share a dirty joke. Yes, the workplace has been wiped of almost all humanity. In some ways this has been good; in others it's bad.

Tell me something nice, you're probably saying. Well, the Red Sox won a World Series. No, I'm serious. They came from three games back against the Yankees to win the pennant. Swear to God the world stood still, and the rivers ran backward. Water became wine. Cats became dogs. It was Shakespeare. It was unbelievable.

You're probably wondering about your beloved Cubs. What can I say? As a kid, you used to sneak into Wrigley to watch them. Now I think that kids are sneaking out. Still, the Chicago Cubs remain enormously popular, one of those things that defies explanation. I don't know if the fans are gloriously faithful or gloriously foolish. But if you see any miracles lying around up there, please send one to the intersection of Clark and Addison.

Politics? Forget politics. If there's a heaven, it's gotta be a place where you can forget politics. But it'll come as no great surprise that rich people are still running the country, new cars are too expensive, and a tank of gas costs a small fortune. You were nothing if not frugal. Decent sedan? Thirty grand. Seriously.

Meanwhile, they're putting heaters inside car seats, and most models come with an optional navigation system that will talk you home. Somehow I think it's best you missed out on that little development. I can just imagine you trying to work the damned thing on the Kennedy Expressway when all you really wanted was the West Coast scores.

When I start listing them like this, it's amazing the things that haven't changed. Doonesbury still stinks. McDonald's can't make a decent hamburger. There's still nothing to watch on television. You would not believe what's become of the sitcom. Yes, they're worse. And the ones you used to scoff at, well, they're making them into movies.

More and more, America seems to pander to the lowest common denominator—in entertainment, in books, in sports, and in food. This wouldn't frighten me so much if the lowest common denominator didn't seem to be getting lower all the time. Instead of raising the bar, we seem to have dropped it to accommodate as many people as possible. We've very inclusive of anyone with 5 bucks in his pocket. Did you ever think such things? I guess dads always do.

Let's see, what else has been happening. Nicklaus just played his last

British Open, and Lance Armstrong just rode his last Tour de France. Who's Armstrong? Well, he's this guy who overcame cancer to win the Tour seven times. I know what you're thinking: "Isn't that just a bike race?" Honestly, I think you would've liked the guy.

Yes, sports has changed. It seems every wide receiver has some gun violation in his past, and every linebacker does cocaine. The agents are running the game, and the head coaches are more like personnel directors than coaches. You think that's a mess, you should see some of the shenanigans they pull in the midget leagues.

Speaking of midgets, the grandkids are good. Your oldest just graduated from college. She has a million ideas a minute and a smile that could light the moon. What she doesn't have is a job. So she's back living with us for a while till she can find something that's a good match for her skills, which are few. I trust that she will be good at anything she tries. You would be so proud.

The boy, meanwhile, has the world on a string. It breaks, and then he ties it back together again. It breaks; he ties it; it breaks. He's got Sinatra's charisma and Steve McQueen's smile. The ladies love him, even if I don't always. What's the deal with teenage boys? On alternate days I want to strangle him or hug him so hard he'll break. You would be so proud.

Meanwhile, the little red-haired girl is the belle of every ball, not to mention a pretty good second baseman. I think she's just like Mom. Not *her* mom, *my* mom—your wife. How scary is that! She has an opinion on everything from the DH rule to Lindsay Lohan's hair. I am not her dad, so much as I am her valet. If she skins her knee, it is somehow my fault. You should see her crush a tennis ball.

The baby? There are no words. Well, there are words, just not enough of them. I took him for a pony ride last week, and you'd have thought he'd won the derby. If I buy him a little football, it's as if he's won the Super Bowl. Talk about "in the moment." He *is* the moment. When music plays, he begins to dance. To him, dogs are demigods, and I am Zeus. Or Ronald McDonald. Last time we picked up a Happy Meal, he pointed to Ronald's picture and asked "Da-da?"

He's vaguely Paleolithic in his personal habits and possesses the tendencies of a nudist. Dressed only in a scarf, he is with me now as I write this, trying to get me to take him to the park.

"Will you close the door when you go?" I ask him. He closes it but doesn't go.

"Oh, you're still here?" I ask.

Yeah, he's still here. They're all still here, a house bursting at its Sheetrock seams with kids and laughter, hissy fits and hair balls. You never warned me that life would be like this. But you showed me how to make the best of it.

Mom? She's good, though I'm pretty sure she still misses you every moment. The house you built still keeps her safe and warm. The gardens you planted still come alive each spring. She's 81 now and no longer mows the lawn herself. What a wimp, huh? If you're worried about her, don't bother. She's tough as timber. On the phone, she still sounds 16.

Dad, if you ever suspect that life is too fleeting—too meaningless, too mundane—you should know that I remember everything you scolded me about and every single word of praise. Of course, I still do some of the things you scolded me about. Hey, I'm a guy.

One last thing. Did I ever say thanks? Did anybody ever say thanks? We all cried when you left, but that's no way to say thanks. The way to say "thank you" is to tell you now how much laughter and comfort you brought to our lives. And to say that it's only after 20 years of going to the office every single day that I can appreciate a guy who did it for 40.

Thing is, I don't think anyone ever really goes away. I feel you around each spring when I plant the tomatoes, or on the occasional afternoon when I wet a fishing line. I remember how much you loved those things, and now I love them, too. I'm taking good care of the tomatoes, and the fish, the kids, and the cars, though frankly I'm reeling in far more tomatoes than rainbow trout.

Let me ask you, Dad, did you prefer live bait or lures? When the tomato leaves turn brown, is that too much water or not enough? Please let me know if you have any tips.

Till then, Jack Daniel's now makes mustard. Down here, the miracles never cease.

12

A WELL-RUN FAMILY MEETING

WE LIVE IN a world that has harnessed the atom but can't seem to stop a 3-year-old from running wild through the Wal-Mart. You can tell a lot about a society by the way it polices its children. With that in mind, I call a family meeting.

"Family meeting!" I yell.

"What?"

"Family meeting!!!"

Usually, what I do at times like these is microwave some popcorn, which makes them think it's midnight and time to get up. Two of them are teenagers, and if it were up to them, they wouldn't be awake during daylight hours at all. If the popcorn doesn't work, I'll open a can of beer.

"Family meeting!" I yell again.

I realized we needed a family meeting after watching the boy consume a sugar donut yesterday—in almost two bites—then brush the sugar from his hands and to the floor as if sugar were a substance that merely evaporates into thin air. It's something normal people would do only while camping. But this kid did it in the middle of the kitchen, in full view of me.

It's moments like this that you fear for the species. Can one little family meeting make a difference? All you can do is try.

"Are we done yet?" the lovely and patient older daughter asks after 30 seconds.

"Not quite," I say, looking at my agenda.

It is a long list, and they know it. It has been a while since we've had a good family meeting. We have a lot of areas to cover.

"Number 1," I say. "Eating a donut."

As I explain to them about sugar donuts, they sit wiggly on the couch, eager for this meeting to adjourn. They look at their watches or examine freckles on their freckly arms. They couldn't be more bored if they were on a 2-year grand jury. Juror number 5, are you awake?

I finish the lecture on sugar donuts by assuring them that there is no substitute for a good hand washing. Germs hate water. I tell them. "Send those germs to Germany," I say, the sort of wit that always delights children.

They don't react. The older daughter pulls on her gum and dangles her legs over the side of the couch. When did she become her mother, I wonder.

"Can't we," the older daughter asks, "just wipe our hands on our T-shirts?"

"Yeah, like you do, Dad," says the little girl.

I don't remember ever doing that. Only a slob would use a T-shirt like a napkin. I know better. I was raised by Republicans.

"You do that all the time, Dad," says the boy.

"I do?"

"Every day," says my wife.

"Keep going, Dad," says the little girl. "You're doing great."

They are a fine audience. The toddler sits on the end of the couch making emu gestures. He's got this new video, you see, and for some reason the movements of the emu really speak to him. He has incorporated the emu into his everyday body language.

Next to him is his 13-year-old sister, who is using her tongue to pluck one of those tiny rubber bands that encircle her braces. Next to her, her older brother is staring at the ceiling, as if hoping for it to fall and crush him. On the end, the lovely and patient older daughter sits calmly with her hands in her lap, holding a key chain with a little cylinder of pepper spray on it. Great, now they're carrying weapons.

"Are we done yet?" she asks.

"We haven't really started," I say.

"When will we be done?" asks the little girl.

"When we're done," I say.

I can see in their eyes that they're impressed with me. "This guy runs a really good meeting," they're thinking to themselves. "Good thing I didn't inherit his chin."

Besides donuts, I caution the four of them about refrigerator etiquette. In truth, we could spend an entire family meeting solely on refrigerator etiquette: how to recognize an empty milk carton and how to close the ketchup, that sort of thing.

My priority today it to stop them from closing the lunch meat drawer with their butts. What they tend to do is open the refrigerator, wipe their lower lips with their wrists in anticipation, then plunge in to the food, grabbing fistfuls of luncheon meat, cheese, and mayonnaise. That's when the trouble begins, because they have, in essence, manacled themselves with food. So, lacking an available hand, they bump the lunch meat drawer closed with their fannies, as if doing an '80s disco dance.

"I would never do that," the older daughter says.

"I've seen you," I say.

"That was somebody else, Dad," says the little girl.

"Butts have germs," I explain. "They should not be used to close lunch meat drawers."

"Whatever," says the older daughter.

I go on to remind them that there is no yelling from the next room. If you're going to yell at someone, walk to the room they're in, then yell.

"Lately, there's been too much yelling," I say.

"Okay, Dad," says the little girl.

I also reiterate our policy on water balloons, namely that water balloons aren't allowed inside the house. If they use them outside the house, they are not to fling them from the roof at passing cars or at old ladies walking dachshunds. For as funny as this sometimes is, it is a rude and obnoxious gesture, and they could hurt their arms.

"I hate water balloons," says the little girl.

"Water balloons suck," says the boy.

"That's the spirit," I say.

We move on to cover couch behavior. I remind them that, in our house, we do not allow young ladies to straddle their boyfriends on the couch as if subduing burglary suspects. If their mother and I ever return home from a movie to find any young ladies doing such things, as we recently did, the young man will be deported, and the young lady will be grounded for a good, long time.

"Grounded?!" sputters our oldest daughter, as if Pepsi went down the wrong pipe.

"Yeah, as in grounded," I say.

Other important household rules I remind them of:

- No drinking straight from the carton.
- No ordering cable movies without parental approval.
- No doodling little heart-shaped symbols at the end of my phone messages.

"That means love, Dad," the little girl explains.

"It does?"

"Not when I do it," says the boy.

"See?" I say.

In fact, they claim to never have done any of the things I mention. They never drink orange juice straight from the carton. They would never, ever order pay-per-view movies on their own.

"Must be other kids, Daddy-O," the older daughter says.

"There are other kids living here?" I ask.

"Probably," says the boy.

It seems unlikely that anybody would live here who didn't absolutely have to. But I suppose there could be other kids residing in our house. Kids come, and kids go, in groups of three or four. The sheer number of handprints on the walls would indicate that at least 20 people live here. Not to mention the $300 grocery bill and socks laying around just anywhere.

"Curfew!" I shout, waking them from their stupors.

"Huh?"

"Curfew is now midnight!" I say, and they grasp their stomachs as if shot.

Like many of today's children, they consider themselves more a board of directors than the hired help they actually are. When someone gives them a direct order, it is their inclination to decline, as if they were turning down an invitation to afternoon tea. "No, thank you. I like my curfew just the way it is, thank you very much."

So to set things straight, I go into other house rules, the ones they once knew but sometimes forget. It never hurts to refresh their little memories. Like most kids, they have a lot on their minds.

- Clear your plates.
- Clean your own room.
- Brush your own teeth.
- When you belch, acknowledge it and excuse yourself to others.

Two things seem to happen when they belch. In the first scenario, they don't even seem to know that it happened. It's as natural as a heartbeat. In fact, they think of it as a heartbeat. One that comes out of their mouths.

Second, they exaggerate the belch into something worse than it actually was, amplifying it in case someone might've been busy and missed it. This is more common with boys than with girls. It is the sort of behavior you see at summer camp, when no parents are around. But sometimes they do it right here in our house. You know, just to get a laugh.

"Oh, and don't forget to use your indoor voices, inside and out," I say.

"That's a good one, Dad," says the older daughter.

"Thanks," I say.

"I don't have an indoor voice," says the boy.

"You do now," I say.

I explain that I have detected a lot of screaming lately in the driveway. Their shrill voices are bound to be driving down home prices. Several neighborhood dogs seem to be losing all their hair. Trees are dropping leaves, dying.

"Are we done?"

"No," I say.

I note to them that church attendance seems to be declining, and that saying a small prayer while watching reruns of *Baywatch* does not constitute a full and spiritual life.

"It doesn't?" asks the boy.

"No," I say.

In fact, it doesn't really qualify as a small prayer, though I am buoyed by the notion that they are praying constantly, even if their prayers mostly involve video games and new clothes. The little girl once prayed 40 times in one afternoon for a pair of Brazilian sandals like the one her little friend Olivia has. When it didn't pan out, she converted to Catholicism, then Judaism. Today, the little girl is full-fledged Buddhist monk and still prays 40 times a day for designer footwear. If nothing else, God must admire her perseverance.

"Did you know," asks the boy, "that if you use the Bible as a coaster, you go straight to hell?"

"You do?" I ask.

"Instantly," says the boy.

"I knew that," says the older daughter.

"You really do?" asks the little girl.

"No more using the Bible as a coaster," I tell them.

"We would never do that, Dad," the boy says.

"I know you wouldn't," I say.

They are a little quieter now, chastened I think by this Bible thing, which came out of the blue. But it was a good point, what the boy said. No one should use religious literature as a coaster. In fact, only self-help books should be used as coasters. And anything written by Nicholas Sparks.

"One last thing . . ." I finally say.

"Finally," sighs the boy.

"Did he say 'finally'?" the older daughter asks.

"And finally . . ." I say.

"What, Daddy?" asks the little girl.

I remind them that watching animated cartoon specials does not constitute honoring Christmas. Christmas is a little deeper than that.

I tell them about some friends whose kids think that the Easter Bunny is Jesus's son. We don't want to ever reach that level of religious confusion. Weekly attendance at church will go a long way to clearing up a lot of their questions about life and giant rabbits.

"Done!" says the boy, bounding to his feet.

"Good meeting, Dad," notes the little girl.

"One last thing," I say.

"We already had a last thing," notes the boy.

"Geeeeesh," says the older daughter, her face like a pretzel.

I tell them, sternly, that I suspect someone has been sipping from the little bottle of butterscotch liqueur in the liquor cabinet. If I find out who, they will be grounded for life, or possibly longer. They will be grounded into the afterlife, and that's no way to begin a good redemption.

"Eternal grounding," the older daughter says. "What could be worse than that?"

I'm stumped for an answer.

Turns out, it was the wife who was sneaking sips of butterscotch liqueur, usually on Friday with her friend Janice, to celebrate the end of another hectic week of kids, carpools, cat vomit, laundry, school projects, soccer practice, and sugar donuts.

"Um, that was me," my wife confesses in front of the group.

I'll deal with her later. Fortunately, in our house, we still allow an occasional spanking.

13

CHEESEBURGERS
AND CHEST EXAMS

SO I'M GETTING my annual physical, a delightful experience I look forward to every 3 years. Here's how it goes: It takes my wife a year to badger me about scheduling my annual physical, and then another year for me to actually get an appointment. I cancel a couple of times, and before you know it, 3 years have passed since my last annual physical. I'm not saying it's the smartest thing.

"How you been?" the doctor asks.

"Oh, fine," I say.

Of course, for the past 45 minutes, I've been sitting in the doctor's chilly office in my underwear, glancing out the window at the cars below while I waited for him to show. I can always pick out the doctors' lot. Porsches, BMWs, Jags. You hear stories about how unhappy doctors are. But they are unhappy in some very nice sets of wheels.

"Been a while," the doctor always says.

"It has?"

"Three years," he says, looking at his clipboard.

"Wow," I say.

He pulls a cold, stainless steel instrument from his pocket. I think he keeps it iced. He puts it on my chest. Then my side. He pulls out another instrument, wooden.

"Say ahhhhh," he says.

"Ahhhhhhh."

"Good," he says.

"Thank you," I say.

I am nothing if not a cooperative patient. If he told me to stand on my head and hum "Stairway to Heaven," I probably would. If he said,

"Throw yourself against the wall, I want to check your motor reflexes," I'd probably do that as well. I trust doctors. Of all the smug, overeducated people I know, I like doctors best.

"Down there, that your Porsche?" I ask.

"Which one?"

"The 911," I ask.

"Yeah, the purple one," he says.

"Like it?"

"Love it," he says.

He asks how I've been. I tell him fine. He checks my ears. Nothing to worry about. He checks down below.

"Cough," he says.

"Cough-cough," I answer.

"Again," he orders.

I tell the doctor that I've been working on a sitcom script about a character with an odd condition. Has he ever run across a man blessed with an extra testicle?

"Three?"

"Yes."

"Well, in a million years of human history," he says, "someone must have had three."

"Smart answer," I say.

"Thanks," he says.

I inform him that the ring finger on my right hand clicks a little. He says there's nothing they can do. Despite all the great medical breakthroughs, they're still working night and day on clicking fingers. I tell him how the other day, my son beat me at basketball for the very first time. Old age, he says. I can tell from his half grin that my annual physical is nearly over.

"Anything else bothering you?" he asks.

Well, since you asked, I hate what the Dodgers' front office is doing. I haven't had a good raise in 5 years. The new neighbors have their cars parked all over the street.

Prime sirloin could be a little cheaper. I'm also concerned that there are too many magazines and that the *New Yorker* is kind of overrated.

And lately, I've been thinking a little too much about the girls I knew in high school. No, you don't understand. *All* the girls I knew in high school, even the ones whose names I didn't know. Back then, some of the girls wore knee socks. I love knee socks. Hey, doc, how come you never see knee socks anymore?

Let's see, what else has been bothering me. Well, if a novel isn't any good, I toss it aside after just 20 minutes and go for a walk instead. The older I get, the more I like my walks. I'm not reflective during these walks. I just walk.

What else. Oh, I wish I could make wine from all the extra tomatoes I have. I wish wishes were hundred-dollar bills.

Incidentally, my wife tells me I clench my jaw when I sleep, and I snore way too much. How I can do both of those things, I don't know. It would seem to be one or the other. No one can snore well with a clenched jaw.

Money is a little tight, and since you asked, my tech stocks haven't been performing all that great. It seems the only decent investment that I have is my house, which seems to increase in value by $100,000 every year. Some years, this equity exceeds my take-home salary. Yet, I have the sneaking suspicion that the money I'm making on the house will be eaten up by taxes and medical costs, weddings, and little sailor outfits for the grandchildren. I can't even imagine the extent to which my wife is going to overindulge the grandchildren. I only know it will be on a significant scale and that Christmases will resemble an ascension to the throne.

That's about all that's bothering me right this minute. But if you like, I could keep a list over the next few days.

What about you, doc? Anything on your mind? No? Good.

Today's men are two things. We think we will live forever, yet we are the first generation to be raised on cheeseburgers and french fries. What a juicy, ketchuped contradiction that is.

So, every morning, I run a little. In the name of good health, I am probably crippling myself. By 60, the cartilage in my knees will resemble corn chips. Still, there I run each morning, on quiet, spooky streets where the front porches never peel. Step-stumble-step. Step-stumble-step. The loneliness of the long-distance dad.

A junkie by nature, I am chasing the little endorphin rush that will get me through the day. If it does my heart and my waistline any good, so be it. Those are mere side effects. What keeps me coming back is the combination of energy and sedative I get from a good, sweaty 40-minute workout. What else would I be doing right now, sleeping? Clenching my jaw? Snoring too loud?

"Faster!" my dopey friends yell from passing cars. "Run faster!"

"Nice to see ya!" I lie.

I don't know what keeps them going. I don't know what their sedative is. In our little town, the Chardonnay and the gin flow like the Colorado River. I indulge, too. A drink or two on weekends. Only occasionally during the week.

The fear of becoming a dysfunctional drinker helps keep me from indulging more often. The thought of having to stop completely is like my drinking muse. Imagine not being able to have a beer during the World Series? Or a glass of wine at a wedding? For me, social drinking is the best drinking.

I drink wisely, in hopes of drinking forever.

Over at the town park, meanwhile, it's busy with these exercise sessions that they've dubbed "boot camp." For about $600, you get a rigorous, 6-week course of exercise and diet, run by goofs dressed like G.I. Joe. Personally, if I wanted to be yelled at by control freaks at 6 in the morning, I'd go to the office. But the boot camps are enormously popular. Like string theory, or Latin, their success is something I'll never really comprehend.

Before sunup, the drill instructors will have a hundred people out there in the wet grass, doing situps and leg lifts. They look to be fashionable sorts, the kind of people tuned to every trend. Up. Down. Up. Down. "Lift those legs, girl!" the drill instructor shouts, and then claps his hands a few times. It is the sort of army you'd put together only if you were going to declare war on, say, Monte Carlo.

But I've seen the results, and they're impressive. My buddy Paul now has a six-pack. It's on his ass, but it's a six-pack nonetheless. Or maybe it's on his forehead. The point is that before this boot camp program, Paul was soft and flabby. He had the only forehead I've ever seen with love handles. For 600 bucks, Paul turned his life around with this silly boot camp. He is far healthier now and occasionally gets lucky. Did I mention that he is a married man? Makes it all the more amazing.

As the father of four, I can't spare 600 bucks. So off I go every morning in my running shoes, on my own, in search of immortality and a healthy buzz.

"Come back to bed," my wife says.

"Gotta run," I say.

"Why?" she moans.

There's a reason they call them the opposite sex. My wife will never really understand my need for exercise, or why I seem to punish myself like this 5 days a week. It's for her. It's for me. It's for all of us. Last time she jacked up the life insurance, I passed the mandatory physical with flying colors. Ha! I'll show her. If this keeps up, I may live to be 49.

In the meantime, my ankles hurt. My lower back stings. I go down hills with the help of gravity and wind; I make it up hills using grit and a certain amount of flatulence. To people who see me jogging, I look like a janitor chasing mice down a flight of stairs. Desperate and sweaty. Agony in motion.

In fact, it is just the reverse. In my mind, I am Jim Brown dropping grenades. Bart Starr scoring over Kramer. Montana finding Rice.

Which brings us, finally, to Sunday. Sweet Sunday.

On Sundays, from October to March, my buddies and I play touch football on the outfield of the local baseball field. Over the 5 years we've done this, the grass has grown thick and healthy with our sweat and blood. From the street, it looks a little like Kentucky bluegrass. Or Augusta after a very moist spring.

"Hut!" someone shouts.

"Huh?"

"I said 'hut,'" the quarterback explains. And then they hike the ball.

Sometimes, this hike goes straight to the quarterback's soft, suburban hands, surprising him with its accuracy. Other times, it soars over his head like a punt, and 10 dads, ranging in age from 35 to 55, chase after the Holy Grail.

Almost always, these games break 100 points in scoring. A typical game ends at 57–55, with the game decided on the very last play. Super Bowls should be so close. Marriage should be so thrilling.

"Out of bounds!" the defensive back rules after a sidelines catch.

"In!" the receiver insists.

"Out!" shouts a linebacker-lawyer.

Yes, there are always a few lawyers present, which means we spend a significant part of the game—usually an entire half—arguing about some minor infraction. This being LA, there are also occasional stand-up comedians, screenwriters, and other fringe-lunatics who make the afternoon bearable.

Those who have been with us awhile play according to their real age. Those who haven't try to play like they are in college again. They always hurt themselves in the second or third quarter. It's pretty funny to watch.

"What happened?" we ask after a hamstring snaps.

"Hammy," the victim whinces, clutching the back of what used to be his leg.

"No kidding," we say, shrugging.

"Maybe you should grow up," someone growls.

What really happened? Well, we got older. Too much time behind the desk. Too many business trips. Too many deadlines, martinis, London broils, seafood platters, cashews, garlic-stuffed olives, Thanksgiving feasts, Christmas chilies, Easter hams. Too many birthdays. Where did they go? Mostly around our waists.

But on Sundays, we are 12 years old again, and the November sun is dropping, and we don't give a damn. The other team is up by 3. Our wives look at the kitchen clocks and wonder where we are. Our dogs wait by the doors.

On Sunday, a receiver streaks down the right sideline, jukes the safety, loses a shoe, bobbles the ball, makes the catch, and tumbles to the turf like a load of dorm-room laundry.

Touchdown.

Tee is up, boys. We're not done yet.

<u>14</u>

IN PRAISE OF PUTTERING

MY HOUSE IS like a sport, too. Mentally challenging. Physically formidable. If you were keeping score, I'd be always behind, always rallying for that late-inning rally. Gutters need cleaning? Of course. Furnace filter need replacing? Yes. If my house were the Yankees, I'd be the Mets. The earnest underdog. A cross-town cupcake.

The person who eventually gets this house will get more than a three-bedroom ranch. He or she will get a door marked with the children's heights—unless of course we take it with us.

He or she will also get a fortune in pennies and nickels that the toddler slips in the pocket door that leads to the bedrooms. He considers this his bank. When the economy collapses, he'll have a good 100 bucks safely stored within the wall. It'll take crowbars to get it out, but that's okay. It's safer there than if the government looked after it.

Any new owner will also get a worn spot in the wood floor in front of the washing machine, where my wife stuffs the clothes, and then pivots on her pretty feet like Margot Fonteyn, wearing out the finish. All the activity has worn down the polyurethane to the point where it is bare wood and scuffed. It looks like Nick Nolte's face after a long summer weekend. In the lab, where they were testing the polyurethane, they likely had no idea that wood floors could ever see this much footwork.

The new owners will get nicks in the woodwork where I brought the Christmas tree into the house. Every January, I'd get out the paintbrush and touch it up, but the wood is dented. The dents are like notches in a bedpost, signs that 15 Christmases happened here.

There's a ping in the fireplace mantel where the boy's fastball once got away from him when he was 12 and demonstrating some pitcher's goofy delivery. It was a strike by the way. Right down the middle.

There are various other dents, bumps, scratches, and bruises, most of

85

them only skin deep. As the handyman here, it is my assignment to repair these signs of trauma. In all honesty, I only get to a few of them.

"Can you look at the garage door?" the woman of the house asks.

"Sure," I say.

I can look at it. I just can't seem to fix it. You hit the button, and the motor sputters for a second, the door jerks down, and then it completely stops. The spiders up high in the timbers go, "Whoa, there he goes again. Where's the Dramamine?"

I hit the button again, and the door grunts, then rocks around, then drops down the way it's supposed to. But it's this initial rocking and pitching I need to fix. If I don't repair it soon, it will shake loose every nail in the house.

Then there's the door that leads out back. It binds a little as you close it. All it takes is an Allen wrench and a few minutes to adjust the hinges. I have the Allen wrench. The few minutes are something else.

"Oh, and don't forget the back door," the wife says.

"It's on my list," I say.

Because I need to get to that utility sink first. It's sitting along the side of the house waiting to be installed. I was going to have it re-porcelained, but as my wife notes, why spend $200 bucks resurfacing something you use to bathe the dog and empty scrub buckets. I can live without a sparkling new utility tub. It's the tomatoes I worry about.

They seem sullen. Not like teenagers, but depressed, you know? When I planted them, I told them stories of all the things they would become: soups, salads, side dishes, pizza. In hindsight, perhaps that was not the thing to do. Perhaps, instead of loved ones, it made them feel like mere crops. But I love my tomatoes, love them with all my mouth.

The peppers could use a little work, too. I think rabbits are nibbling them at night while we sleep, perhaps even while I type you this. I hope it gives them gas. I hope they have trouble sleeping. For I love my peppers. Almost as much as I love my eggplant.

The eggplant is completely AWOL. I planted it from seeds, and while the cucumbers, radishes, and pumpkins seem to be doing well all around it, the eggplant has yet to tuft up through the ground. I don't know what I'll do about the eggplant. Thank God, I've got good kale.

There are certain things that begin to bedazzle you as you age, inexplicably and without warning. Baseball, I think is one of them. Its pace and history seem to appeal more as you get older. Hard liquor is another. Never had the tongue for it when I was younger. Now, I cherish the occasional sip. Cigars. Golf. Jazz. Gardening. Let us honor our middle-aged lovers.

"Dad, can I help?" the little girl asks.

"No."

"Please?"

"Okay, grab that shovel," I say.

She will not last long. They never last long. To a kid, there is no immediate payoff in gardening, no buzz of conquest. They are raised on video games and microwaves. What's so cool about something you can't see move? Heck, you can't even plug it in.

I explain to her how the tomatoes thrive if you strip them of their lower leaves. I show her how we have to stake them, to give them places to hang out. I make gardening fun for her. I make it irresistible.

"I'm going inside," she says after 15 minutes.

"You didn't weed the peppers," I tell her.

"I think I hear the phone," she explains, breaking into a run.

There is majesty in gardening, but you don't need me to tell you that: Faith and majesty are best left undescribed. They are internal reactions. As you get older, you realize that some of the best rewards don't elicit handsprings or high-fives. Our best rewards can be a quiet contentment. Soup. Reading. Children.

The boy wanders by. He has a project of his own. He is taking an old surfboard and creating a coffee table from it. He's got my old banana yellow board. And some scrap wood he found in a neighbor's junk pile. From this, he will craft a base for the surfboard.

"Need help?" I ask.

"No," he says.

"Sketch out your base first," I urge.

"Okay," he says.

There is something about a little project that lets us discover ourselves. I don't know that the boy can really make a table. Such carpentry skills seem to have eluded our family the way brassieres eluded Lady Godiva. Yet, let him try. Let him make his own mistakes.

"Call if you need a hand," I say.

"Thanks, Dad," he says and disappears into my workshop.

On the porch stands their mother, the toddler at her side. My wife is holding his arm a little too high, so that only one of his feet is fully touching the ground. It is the same way a sheriff holds the town vagrant. If you read body language, this means that she has had her fill of him in some way. I find that hard to imagine. But I've heard it happens.

"Can he come out?" my wife asks.

"No," I say.

"He wants to come help," she explains.

"Help!" the toddler says.

"Okay, come on out," I tell him.

He runs to me as if ablaze.

Of all the kids, a toddler is probably the most useful in the garden. Enthusiastic and highly untrainable, he will leave the weeds and pick the real stuff. He will water your shoes. If you're not paying attention, he will rake your head.

"I'm glad you came along," I tell him.

"No problem," he says, adding more manure to my shoe.

I give him a spray bottle and turn him loose on the tomato plants. Even for him, a man of unlimited dedication and energy, it is difficult to overwater a tomato plant with a mere spray bottle. It should take him years. I turn to see him spritzing the weeds.

"No, not the weeds," I say.

"No?"

"The tomatoes," I tell him.

I remind him how the tomatoes are the most important crop we have. He's an old soul trapped in a shiny new fuselage. I trust he'll understand.

"You like tomatoes?" I ask him. "Wait till you taste them grilled."

"Hmmmmm," he says, rubbing his belly.

This is one of our little schticks. I say "tomatoes," and he responds by rubbing his belly and saying "Hmmmmmmmm." I have seen it work at dinner parties and ballgames. He is Rowan to my Martin. Cosby to my Culp. Every man should have such a sidekick.

"And pizza," I say. "Wait till you taste fresh tomatoes on pizza."

"Hmmmmmm," he says.

"That's the spirit," I tell say.

I could grill your oldest boots and have them come out edible. Give me a dozen cigar butts, and I will baste them and char them till you have hors d'oeuvres. I'm pretty sure that there is something about pure flame that brings the most appetizing qualities from any object. Don't throw out that old suitcase. I'll just grill it.

The plants around the grill seem to thrive more than others. Perhaps it's the heat from the Kenmore grill, or the barbecue sauce I toss around while basting. It is the most fertile ground we have. I'm pretty sure, given enough sunlight, I could raise redwoods from its moist loam.

The toddler and I till the ground for 30 minutes. I pull out the last clover of spring and snatch up a few dandelions. The toddler pulls some radishes that were not yet ripe.

"Hmmmmmm," he says when I tell him about the salads we'll have. "Hmmmmmm," he purrs when I mention tomatoes.

"Is he okay out here?" my wife asks.

"He just dug up my peppers," I tell her. "And you should see what he did to the radishes."

The radishes were to be our real cash crop. They are the only vegetable in our garden that grows faster than the weeds. I suspect that in a radish's heart, he thinks he is a weed. There is nothing in his appearance that would tell him different.

When the radishes took hold early in the spring—blanketing their small area and growing inches each day—I envisioned setting up a radish stand in the front of the house, a rickety old wooden thing where I could put my feet up, smoke a pipe, and sell tray after tray of beautiful radishes all afternoon. I'd create a radish fever in Los Angeles, which always seems preoccupied with those horrible action-adventure movies they make now.

Something as pure and simple as a radish craze would soothe the city's long-dormant spirit.

"Radishes! Get your radishes!" the kids would scream as cars lined up. We'd sell salt, too.

"They're great on salads," I'd explain. "Or you can eat them plain."

The poor radish could use a boost. You don't see them on salads so much anymore. And salad bars seem to be not so much in vogue.

So it's up to us to stoke radish futures. Like soybeans, there must be an index.

"Maybe he should come in?" my wife suggests, the baby having stomped the radish patch with his little size 4 shoes. By this, I think he thought he was motivating them to do better.

"He's all right," I say. "Radishes always bounce back."

The toddler plays with roly-polies a while. These are his real passion, the hard little bugs that curl up in the palm of your hand. Roly-polies are, virtually, toddler-proof. He gets an old mustard jar and adds some leaves and grass and about a dozen roly-polies.

After the garden, we work on the window screens, sudsing them up, and then spraying them with a hose. It's not as complicated as it sounds.

From the screens, we move on to turning down the hot water heater—summer's coming—and changing out the furnace/air-conditioning filter. It is filled with lint and the hair of four children.

From there, we take on the dog's ears. The poor cocker spaniel has those long ears that droop like Spanish moss along the sides of his head. No air gets in, so his head becomes a house of wax. He gets pounding ear-aches. As you know, there are few things sadder than a dog in discomfort.

"Let's fix Lucky," I tell the toddler.

"What's wrong?" he asks.

"His ear is gooey," I say.

"Sounds serious," he says.

"It'll work out."

The dog does a lap dance on my legs as I try to clean his ears. First, I use a Q-tip soaked in alcohol. I follow that with a cotton ball. Such intimacy leaves the little dog both grateful and aroused. Seldom does love run this deep. I make a mental note to save some cotton balls for later.

"Who loves ya?" I ask the little dog.

"You do," he groans, his rear leg kicking as I clean his ear.

"Who loves ya?" I ask the toddler, who's squirming and splayed across my shoulders.

"You do," he says.

"Better believe it," I say.

Whoever gets our house, gets all this. Handprints on the wall as folk art. An aging sprinkler system. A dishwasher that occasionally over-flows.

It's not much. But we really liked it.

15

SLEEPING WITH A SOCCER MOM

I'D LIKE TO THINK I am a somewhat sophisticated man—a college grad, a connoisseur of good literature and decent wine (when it's on sale). Yet, here I am on a Friday night planning a soccer game between eager, indulged children as if it were the Battle of Antietam.

Brittany on defense? No, Brittany at forward. Madison at sweeper? No, Madison at mid. Madison has Soccer Attention Deficit Disorder (SADD). In mid-kick, just as she's about to finish her backswing and bring her pink, $60 soccer shoe forward, a dragonfly buzzing over the field will draw little Madison's attention away from the task at hand. She will stop, smile at the dragonfly, hike up her droopy shorts, and then stop to think about what she was doing before the dragonfly dropped in to say hello. We'd better keep Madison at midfield. She's SADD.

"Madison's a good sweeper," her mother assured me after the second practice, and even though Madison's mom is pretty good-looking, one of those divorcees who really takes care of herself—2 hours in the gym, tight-fitting tops, etc.—I try not to notice such things.

"Every position is open," I tell her, glancing only momentarily at her lovely, surgically endowed chest. There are da Vincis still among us, but their sculpture is restricted to noses, necks, and chests. Eventually, there will be no ugly people left but me.

Till then, I am immune to such beauty, for I am already sleeping with one of the mothers on the team. She's a little redhead, the mother of one of my star players. Before you get all self-righteous and moral, let me assure you that we're both aware of the consequences. Besides, it's a very common coaching fantasy that you'll someday be rewarded for all the hard work with the passion of one of the player's moms. Want to know what's even kinkier? We're married. Sick but true.

Of course, in this case, she doesn't sleep with me because I'm the coach. She sleeps with me out of habit and a sense of resignation. For nowhere in our wedding contract, which allows for individual growth and odd behavior, was there ever anything about her having to share me with the sport of soccer. Our prenup was more along the lines of:

- If you make a mess, clean it up.
- If you get fat, so will I.
- No watching TV all day like some lazy slug.

That, for the most part, was our prenuptial agreement. It carried no guidelines on money, or who would get the house because we didn't really have one. Most prenups have some sort of morals clause. Not ours. Basically, if you showed up each night, the other partner would have to take you back in.

It certainly didn't mention soccer, Little League, or the role sports in general would play in our imperfect union. Nowhere was there any language about being late to Thanksgiving dinner when the Packers were driving and all they needed was a field goal to tie. "Oh-my-God, look at the pass Farve threw! Oh-my-God, he's going for the touchdown!" Nowhere did it mention that.

Nor did it mention that once we had kids of a certain age, our weekends would be devoted to traveling to far-off fields in a minivan, to play teams we'd never met before. Or that Saturday night would be spent in the easy chair, trying to get blood back into our ankles and recovering from heatstroke and dehydration, because the next day you were going to do it all over again. In a perfect world, such acknowledgments would be part of every marriage contract.

When my wife said "I do," in that hot little Florida church, she had no idea what she was in for, sports wise. Since then, I've lined fields by moonlight. I've coached triple-headers in the desert heat. I've given up my sweatshirt during cold rainy soccer games when, at halftime, the kids couldn't talk because their teeth were chattering so badly.

I've stood in the middle of huddles, enduring the fetid breath of 10 players—Doritos, chocolate milk, gum, Tootsie Rolls, you wouldn't believe the crap they consume—and drawn out plays on a dry erase board that won't really erase anymore. Other times, I've sketched plays on my own hand, not realizing I was using permanent marker.

The family limo—a minivan—often resembles a rolling garage sale. On right turns, balls roll out from under the seats. On left turns, they roll back underneath. When we finally trade it in, it will come with seven baseballs we know are there but can't find. A soccer pump or two. And a big black carpet stain that looks like an oil spill but is really a melted cylinder of eye black.

Our minivan has seen more ball games than Tommy Lasorda. There are sunflower seeds in the cup holders and that god-awful Gatorade on all the window switches. It's a mess, really. It is now so sticky it repels warm water and detergent of any kind. Touching it with your hand is like sticking your tongue to an icicle. It refuses to let go.

But I will admit this: Some of the best moments of parenthood have been spent with this minivan packed with soccer players or softball pitchers, on the way to pizza after the game, their voices so shrill that I fear they might somehow deploy the airbags or shatter the windshield.

"Sit down and shut up," I'd yell, when what I really meant was, "Sit down and never grow up." The Lost Boys of my children's youth.

"Rain? Yes!" my wife says.

"But we have a game tomorrow," I plead.

"We could use a day off," she explains.

Nearly every season, we reach that point. My wife prays for rainouts. I pray that we'll play. It is a source of endless friction. I've waited all week for some silly little game. She just wants to sleep till 8. Sometimes, I fear my wife has Soccer Attention Deficit Disorder. How ironic is that? It's a little like Beethoven losing his hearing.

"Why," she asks, "do they have so many games?"

"I always thought we could use more," I tell her.

Admittedly, most kiddy sports seasons are too long. It's become even worse for those kids playing on "travel" or "club" teams, which our family has avoided like the chicken pox. Players on these teams, formed from the very best players in each town, face year-round seasons and unreasonable expectations. In typical American fashion, these teams have taken something that's inherently pure and decent—kids playing ball—and turned it into a career path. Now every town has a club team that travels far and wide to play other such all-star teams in hopes that little Kara will earn a scholarship to Arizona or Fresno State.

"I'm telling you right up front," coaches of such teams say. "This isn't just about fun." Amazingly, parents nod and agree to participate.

So I am sympathetic to setting limits in youth sports. I am also sympathetic to anything that will keep husbands out of hot water with the soccer moms with whom they share a house and a bed. There's hot water everywhere these days. If you're not careful, you will drown and boil at the same time.

To young husbands everywhere, I would offer these youth sports prenups. Keep in mind that these are only guidelines. Sensible husbands should also consult an attorney and, possibly, an undertaker.

Coaching Prenup Agreement:

- Never sign up to coach without a notarized signature from your spouse and a note from a psychiatrist.
- Always acquire written agreement from your employer that it's okay to duck out of work at 4 p.m. to get to the field in time to chalk it. That way, when you are fired a month later, you'll have grounds for some sort of severance.
- Be sure to seek dispensation from certain birthdays and anniversaries that are bound to be spent, not in a fine restaurant or a fancy spa, but in a dusty, gopher-riddled baseball park where hot dogs are a buck and slushees 50 cents. "Happy 10th anniversary, honey," you'll say. "I got you these nice nachos."
- Notify your wife in advance that your entire social life will now be based on the parents you meet at baseball, soccer, basketball, or hockey, as limiting as that can sometimes be.
- Acknowledge in advance that if your kid's team gets hot during the playoffs and advances through regional, sectional, and state tour-

naments, you will hock your wedding rings, cash in your 401ks, and sell your blood in order to pay for the family to fly to Williamsport, or Spokane, or some other one-cop town, for the national finals. It makes no sense. But you will.

- Ask permission to spend hour upon hour on the phone and the computer, reminding families of the upcoming game, or filing game reports, or exchanging e-mails with the other coaches about some ridiculously petty injustice that has just taken on the significance of Roe v. Wade.

- Accept that the biggest day of the year will no longer be Christmas or Easter, but draft night, where a dozen coaches will sit on creaky chairs for 3 hours, divvying up a couple of hundred kids to various teams. The Treaty of Versailles did not require this kind of concentration. At one point, several people will no doubt come to blows.

If a young couple can abide by this sort of agreement, they are destined for great fun on the ball fields of America. If they can't, they are headed for 10 years of arguments, meltdowns, flare-ups, and never-ending tension. Granted, it can be a little hard to tell the difference.

In the meantime, I am sleeping with a soccer mom. I don't recommend it to everybody. But I find soccer moms quite appealing. I love the way they look with lawn chairs on their shoulders and toddlers clinging to their knees. They stay fit, many of them. They always bring good snacks.

I find mine in bed, reading, as I crawl in a little after 11. I just couldn't seem to get that game lineup the way I wanted. Then Tiffany's dad called and said she might have the flu, he wasn't sure. So I had to make two lineups, one with Tiffany and one without. Under this kind of pressure, a lot of guys would crack. But I'm more than a man. I'm a soccer coach.

I am reminded that women, for unfathomable reasons, find fathers who spend time with their kids very appealing. It's one of those perks they never tell you about in the coaches clinics. Sexy may not be the right word. "Hot" certainly doesn't cover it. But, within the female kingdom, the devoted dad has a certain unexpected cache. Honestly, I'd rather be considered hot.

Once in bed, our conversation goes like this:

Me: Heavy sigh.
Her: Heavy sigh.
Me: Tiffany might be sick.
Her: Which one's Tiffany?
Me: The sick one.
Her: You take this way too seriously.

She goes on to describe how the night before, she awakened me from a restless dream. I was disoriented and a little sweaty. When she asked me who I was dreaming about, I told her soccer. I explained that I try to pre-play most games in my head, just to get my strategy down. It's the reason for so much of my coaching success.

Her: You're a little obsessed.
Me: You can't be a little obsessed.
Her: You can't?
Me: Either you're obsessed or you're not.
Her: Then you're obsessed.
Me: You could be a little more supportive.
Her: Heavy sigh.
Me: Heavy sigh.

She closes her book. She turns out the light. It is quiet. I am thinking what every husband thinks at moments like this. Is that all? Is she just going right to sleep?

Me: Can I ask you something?
Her: Huh?
Me: At goalie, would you play Caitlin or Bree?

There is a long pause. You'd have thought I asked her to marry me all over again. That would require some thought.

Her: Bree.
Me: Thanks.
Her: Or Caitlin.

If you ask me, she's a little obsessed.

16

The Lovely and Patient Older Daughter

MY DAD ASKED me to write a chapter of his book, on account of when I write his column for him occasionally, he gets all these e-mails saying what an accomplished writer I am and that he'd better watch out because there's someone better in the wings waiting to take his place.

"Maybe," I told him, "I should write the whole book?"

"Maybe not," he said.

"I could be your Cyrano," I said.

"Just start writing," he said.

My dad's been so busy lately. First, he's been writing this book. Sometimes, he spends up to 20 minutes at a stretch in front of the computer, drinking black coffee and combing his hair with his fingers. He'll stop a while and scratch his back with a pencil. Then he flicks off the computer and goes out to the garage. What he usually does in the garage is move a lot of things around, and then move them back. Mom knows what he's doing the whole time, trying to make her think he's really accomplishing something. I swear, it's a total scam. Every time she opens the door he's, like, on the garage couch, reading an old *Esquire* or snoring.

"Taking a little break?" she asks.

"My back hurts," he explains.

"Poor baby," my mom says.

"And my front isn't doing so hot either," he says.

"Want me to rub it?" she asks.

"Dumb question," he says.

"DAAAAAAD!" I scream, because there are still a lot of young kids around.

Sometimes, it's like my mom and dad are on their first date. Sometimes, it's like they may never speak again. Dad says this is very typical of California marriages.

He says that, for him, this is just a "starter marriage" anyway and that he expects to have three or four more happy marriages before it's over. I tell him that he's lucky to have found even one woman who would marry him. Seriously, he still listens to Boz Scaggs albums. You should see the jeans he wears.

And you should see him right now reading the newspaper. It's very appealing. My dad is the only person I know who burns up calories just by reading the news. He grunts and flails his arms and rubs the frustration out of his face. It's sort of like when he does the taxes.

"Did you see this?!!!" he'll scream suddenly at the front page, or, "Oh, those stinkin' Dodgers . . ." It's as if he's wrestling with the paper instead of reading it. He hasn't even hit the editorial page yet.

The other day, he was going off that there were too many prepositions in the paper and that most prepositions can be eliminated just by recasting a sentence a little.

"We might not need prepositions at all," he said. "You ever think of that?"

"All the time, Dad," my brother said.

"Tell me more about the parts of speech, Daddy," said my suck-up little sister.

"There are too many adverbs, too," my dad said, and she just beamed.

This from a man who spent one morning talking completely in rhyme, sort of like that dude Jesse Jackson. My dad says it's on account of having read too many bedtime books to his four kids, and that rhyming just gets stuck in his head sometimes. He tells Mom that the only way he can stop is if she makes him a big, gloppy sandwich.

"I'd really like ham, and I don't mean SPAM," he tells her.

"Okay, enough with the stupid rhymes," Mom says.

"I'm going to be cool, because I'm nobody's fool," he answers back.

"Enough!" she yells.

It's easy to see why he's such a huge success. Do you know that we haven't had a new car in, like, 5 years? My mom is driving the exact same car she was driving when I went off to college 4 years ago. It's this big, ugly minivan. I say, "Hey, Mom, why not a farm tractor? Why not a mail truck?"

Do you know how embarrassing that is . . . a 5-year-old minivan in LA? The paint on the luggage rack, it's peeling. And the vinyl on the bumpers isn't looking so hot, sort of scuffed and stuff, on account of my brother learning to drive. When I point this out to my dad, he just shrugs and swigs more coffee.

"That car carries a lot of memories," he says.

"Good ones?" I ask.

"Like the day we took you off to college," he says.

"Bad ones, too," my mom says.

"Yeah, like when you came back," my dad says wistfully, and then lets out a big breath, as if he'd been keeping it in for several years and is finally just now exhaling. It's, like, air from 2002.

I can't believe I'm back living at home. College was so great. In college, you have two or three classes a day, that's it, and tons of reading that you don't really have to do. As if anybody's gonna really read *Ulysses*?

I loved college. It's set up to be this sort of guilt-free environment. No one tells you when to get up or when to go to sleep. I went a whole week once eating organic waffles, that's all.

Plus in college, you can just sort of give yourself a day off when you need it to go to the beach. Or you can get Starbucks and go to the library and crash a while in the big, comfy chairs they have there. I swear, at our college, the library was like one big bed where everybody slept. Seriously, I'm thinking of going to grad school.

"How's the job hunt going?" my dad says every day when he gets home from work.

"Tomorrow, Paramount," I say.

"Studios?"

"No, Paramount auto insurance," I say. "Of course the studios."

"Wow, good luck," he says, and then goes to my brother's room to yell at him. When you have a teenager, I guess you do a lot of yelling. The kids never really hear you. I think it's mostly for the parents to blow off steam and stuff.

"Where you going, Dad?" I ask.

"To yell at your brother," he says.

"What'd he do?"

"Nothing yet," he says. "It's more a preemptive thing."

"Yell at him for me, okay?" I ask.

"Will do," says my dad.

Oh-my-God, my dad and my brother are so weird. The other day, they had a very serious discussion, where my brother came right out and told my dad face to face that he was now a Yankees fan. My dad stormed out of the bedroom and screamed at my mom.

"A Yankees fan?" he said. "Not in my house, a Yankees fan."

Then my parents argued for maybe an hour about the symbolism of someone choosing the mighty Yankees, when they were raised to worship the Cubs and the world's other great underdogs, like the Chicago Bears or the UPN network. My mother said my dad has to learn to be more tolerant of oddball belief systems and crazy lifestyles.

"These kids, they'll kill me with disappointment," my dad said at one point.

"I'm a Yankees fan, too," said my little sister.

"No!" screamed my dad.

"Yes, I am!" she giggled, and he chased her around the kitchen.

Oh-my-God, do you see all the fun we're having? Do you see why I need a job so I can get out of here immediately? I swear, if I knew I was going to be living back home again, I would've taken way more psychology classes in college.

"My id is feeling a little odd," my dad told me the other day when I mentioned psychology.

"No kidding," I said.

"But my mojo has never been better," he said.

Oh. My. God.

102

17

WHAT TO DO
WITH AN EMPTY NEST

AS A MAN of vision—a man who shuns sentiment and looks only forward, never back—I think often of eventually opening a bed-and-breakfast. It won't be till our golden years, when we're looking to refill our empty house. This gives us plenty of time to plan. To determine the pitfalls. To do things right.

"You want to open what?" my wife asks.

"A clothing-optional B&B," I tell her.

"Clothing optional?"

"Yes," I say.

"Great," she says, but I sense she doesn't really mean it.

For she is forming a little crescent with her mouth that you see when she is sampling the half-and-half to see if it's gone sour. The laugh lines disappear, and then blend into a frown. It is not her most flattering expression, though I find in it traces of Rembrandt. Of mystery and nuance and all the things that make great art.

"You know what you'd have?" she asks.

"What?"

"People like Doris Roberts," she says.

"Who?"

"Doris Roberts," she says, "the one on *Raymond*."

I knew she'd come around to the idea. She just needed to chew on it awhile. But if she's picturing Doris Roberts naked in our living room, there may be hope for this B&B concept yet.

As she pouts, I remind her that I am a man of vision. Where others spot weeds, I see wildflowers. Where others see naked old sitcom actresses, I see a nice bottom line.

"Careful, Copernicus," she says. "You'll burn the toast."

I butter the toast and explain to her that guests wouldn't have to be naked. It would only be an option. Say you were sunbathing or eating a scone, you could shed your shirt or pants and let the summer breezes caress your buttermilk skin. Our backyard is pretty private. No one but us and a few squirrels would have to know.

"That's a pretty big but," she says.

"There'd be lots of big buts," I say.

"I can't believe," she says, "that you'd want to do it here."

Granted, most B&Bs are housed in nice old Victorian homes, with cotton curtains on the windows and doilies on the antique tables. But we have antiques, too. You should see my dress shoes.

And why not here, in our little suburban ranch? Why not on the cul-de-sac, in suburban LA? The majority of B&Bs open in remote places like Oregon or Vermont, areas prone to cattle stampedes and bee stings. Our guests will be safer here. We could guide them to the drugstore or to Hollywood Boulevard. We'd give them tips on when best to go to Disneyland or how to avoid a carjacking. In the evenings, we'd relax over wine and cheese. If people felt comfortable, they would be free to shed their moo-moos and their Keds.

"It's just something to think about," I tell her.

"What about them?" she asks, nodding toward the children.

Oh, them. Well, eventually, all children have to leave, right? They can't just live here forever, though with today's housing prices the chances of them affording anything within 100 miles are slim. But in another 30 or 40 years, I expect them to be out of our hair. We'll bring in some new furniture and. . . .

"Yewwwwwww," our older daughter says when she gets wind of the B&B idea. "That's just so . . . yewwwwwwwww."

You'd expect a college-aged kid to be more receptive to nudity, given that when they bend down their underwear always sticks out. In kindergarten, they were scolded not to go around showing their underwear to just anybody. Now, when they turn 13, their backsides become billboards. They favor skimpy tops and kite string underwear. Basically, when they leave the house, they are wearing less than when we birthed them.

"I thought you'd be more open-minded," I tell her.

"Has Dad been watching Cinemax again?" my daughter asks her mom.

"Every night," she tells her.

"I'm just a sucker for a love story," I explain.

But back to our B&B for a second. This isn't some golden years indulgence. It'd be a viable money-maker. By then, the corporate goons will have raided all our pensions. Social Security will just be some question on a history test. We'll need to pay for our Lipitor some way.

I explain that our B&B would be called "Romeo and Juliet's" in honor of the love that flourishes here. We'd hang a shingle in Old English out on the porch and plant some morning glories to climb all over it. Hang an old American flag, with an eagle on the flag stick.

I'd take care of the breakfasts. My wife would take care of the beds. I figure that the boy's bedroom at the far end of the house will be perfect for the guests. It has its own full bath. We'd just have to get the pet smells out of the carpets. And the Scotch Tape marks off the walls from all his snowboarding posters.

"I'm not leaving," explains the boy.

"Seriously?"

"Seriously," he says.

In truth, I fear that they are never leaving. I stand in the middle of the big kitchen, cooking scrambled eggs and toast and the thought occurs, "Why would they ever leave?" Someone does their sheets. Someone does their eggs. They never run out of toilet paper, towels, or milk. In fact, there is a giant fridge, big as a Buick, always full of food, some of it still a little fresh.

"We've already done it," I tell my wife.

"Done what?"

"Opened a B&B," I say. "Except it's for them."

My wife turns to glance at the kids. One is putting cream cheese on her M&M's. Another is applying eye shadow to the dog. The toddler is French-kissing the cat. The realization that we are operating a B&B for kids quiets my wife, a rare moment of reflection in a life that doesn't allow for much. That little trace of Rembrandt? It's back.

For, in many ways, I am right. We're a B&B. Except we're never paid. Never thanked. No one calls ahead if they're going to be a little late. No one looks you in the eye when you speak. It's not exactly the nice Vermont B&B life you used to see on *Newhart*.

"Dad?" asks the little girl.

"Huh?"

"Can you make me a crepe?" she asks.

"Sure," I say.

See how easily we fall victim to their needs? We are martyrs to our children. Money that we once spent on romantic getaways, we now spend on the latest shoes, which they wear twice, and then shove to the back of the closet with the $80 ski sweatshirts they just had to have but never wear. The money we were saving for retirement now goes to some gigantic state university with 30,000 students and dorms as nice as Marriotts.

"How come," I ask my wife, "elementary school is free, but state college now costs, like, $8,000 a minute?"

"I don't know," she says, but you can tell she hasn't given it much thought. I think she's still dwelling on the mental image of some Doris Roberts type sitting naked on our new couch while discussing her disappointing lunch at Spago . . . that the only celebrity she saw was Potsie from *Happy Days* . . . the shrimp in her salad were lukewarm. That kind of stuff.

"How's my crepe coming?" the little girl asks.

"Great," I say.

Actually, her crepe is coming out a lot like a pancake, since the innkeeper has never made a crepe before. My cooking skills are restricted to Jiffy Pop and anything involving ground beef. Chili. Meatballs. Tacos. My next book will be titled *Cooking with Grease*. When you open it, it'll smell like a Taco Bell.

I am just now, in fact, learning to use the kitchen. For years, I could cook almost any kind of meat on the barbecue grill out under the olive trees. Chicken. Flank steak. Chops. I was the King of Kabobs. Master of All Meat.

Then I added vegetables to my menu. I could blacken asparagus over high flame—if you haven't tried it, you should—and all sorts of other vegetables, too. I'd spend long summer nights with a beer in one hand and tongs in the other. They'd sort of balance each other out: beer and tongs. As I finished my beer, I'd begin to list like a sailboat.

"Quick, get him another beer!" friends would say. "Before he falls over."

If you asked me my favorite moment of the entire week, it was those moments out under the olive trees—beer in one hand, tongs in the other. I'd watch the sun set and the trees disappear into the inky night. In the bushes, the raccoons would stir from their daylong slumber. "What'd he drop on the ground this time?" they'd wonder. "I hope it's ribs tonight."

I long to run a restaurant with just one table. I'd do all the cooking and drinks myself. I'd have a staff of one to clear the table and do the dishes. Maybe a chesty hostess to take names at the door and repeat over and over, "It'll be just a few more minutes," when in fact she knows it'll be far longer. If she's chesty enough, I figure half the diners won't care. I don't want to rush people. The best part of a great dinner is the afterglow.

With that in mind, I'm learning to cook in the kitchen as well. As you may have noticed, after a certain age—usually around 50—husbands take over a lot of the routine cooking chores. I don't know what the wives take over. I'm eager to find out and encourage them along.

"Anybody want a pancake?" I ask.

"I ordered crepes," says the little girl.

"Well, you're getting pancakes," I tell her.

"Okay, Daddy," she says.

Parenthood is the longest march. A life sentence, really. One day leads to the next, one atop the other. You don't notice the kids growing older. Elementary school seems to go on for 20 years. Then they hit junior high and off to the races they go. They will no longer look at you, but they will be drawn to every mirror or reflective surface they see. There are not enough mirrors in all the world for a 13-year-old girl. They move from one reflective surface to the next. Mirrors, shiny cars, the crystal of a watch. If a 13-year-old goes 2 minutes without seeing her reflection, she may very well explode.

CHRIS ERSKINE

A year or two later, they are driving and dating. Notice how so many parental minefields begin with the letter "D"? Driving. Dating. Dorms. Divorce.

Before you know it, they are heading off to college. Who knows what they're doing then? You know only that you are funding it all. Toga parties and keggers. For the first 18 years, they are expected to behave within the constraints of a good Republican suburb. Then you take them off to college and you worry that they'll never bathe again. And if they do, will it be alone?

Then, in no time, they're getting married, another thing you'll finance, and they begin to think about a family of their own. Ouch. They don't need a family. They've got us. US! Don't you remember who raised you? It was US!

I don't even want to think of such things yet. For, when they're caring for their own kids, whom will we care for? Ourselves? Get out. All that training, just to take care of each other? Surely, we'll need other responsibilities. We'll need a decent B&B. Or maybe we'll open a kennel.

"I'll have an omelet," says the boy.

"Do we have any bagels?" asks the older daughter.

On second thought, maybe we should skip the breakfasts and just open a bed. We'll hang out a shingle and call it "The Grateful Bed." No breakfasts, just beds. Guests would get up, go out for breakfast, and then begin their day touring the wonderful sights of Los Angeles. In the evening, they'd return to find a nice bed and a clean towel.

Might work. It'll keep us occupied, if nothing else. And that whole naked thing? That'd be completely optional.

18

HEY, KIDS,
KEEP OFF THE GRASS!

I THINK IT'S GOOD the way children never play outside anymore. There they would be exposed to fresh air and sunlight, the beauty of a tree. Birdsong and cloud formations. Moon glow and apple trees. Yes, the outdoors is no place for kids.

Each morning, I drive past great lawns of winter rye trod upon only by the strangers hired to mow and rake them. They are beloved by dogs, that's all.

The last time I saw a kid mow a lawn was 1987, and I'm not sure even to this day whether he was a real kid or merely an apparition. He might've been like those figures in *Field of Dreams*, a ghostlike vision who emerged from the cornfields of my imagination. Regardless, I have seen nothing like it since.

Once, kids had no choice but to go outside, kicked out of the house by grouchy parents tired of their fussing and horseplay, or the very sound of Don Knotts's voice on TV ("Geez, Andy, how was I supposed to know the gun was even loaded?").

We were banished to the out of doors, the best punishment a kid ever had. We'd go days in the Illinois summer—possibly weeks—without putting on shirts or shoes. At night, the bottoms of our feet would be so dirty that they wouldn't come clean. By the end of summer, the bottoms of our feet were so leathery that you could step on a hot stick and barely even notice. Shoes would've been redundant.

The driveway was our chief gathering place. Our union hall. Our lab. We'd burn ants with magnifying glasses and make bows and arrows from string and willow branches. We'd go on long hunting expeditions for rabbit and squirrel. I once shot a rabbit point blank in the local cemetery. The arrow, whittled with a pen knife, bounced off his shank like a moth off a window screen, and the rabbit went gliding off into the brush, probably to tell all his friends. For rabbits, great stories like that don't come along every day.

When we weren't hunting, we were experimenting. We launched water rockets. We flew kites. On the hottest summer days, we'd have internecine water balloon fights that would leave at least one kid with a giant red welt on his back, as if spanked. It's amazing no one drowned.

We'd spend other days flying balsa wood gliders. The gliders would land on roofs and in the trees. We'd rescue them, and then send them back up again. We'd spend other days popping little powder-filled caps with rocks. Pop-pop-pop. The rolls of caps were made to be used in toy guns, but smacking them with rocks was far more fun. Pop-pop-pop.

My sidekicks were a charming if grimy lot. There was Rob, an orphan with parents. He had parents, only we never saw them. We'd go to his house for sleepovers and never see any sign of adult supervision. Rob told us his parents were always working, but we just assumed Rob and his seven brothers—yes, seven—had the parents bound and gagged some-where in the basement. How else could the cereal be always out. The TV always on. The beds never made. Rob's house was, we thought, pretty much the best place on Earth.

There were also the twins, Jim and Joe. Jim was the edgy one, Joe a little nicer. Naturally, Jim got most of the girls.

There were neighbor girls whose names I don't remember, though I recall hearing one had a big mole right on her butt.

And I remember Andy, the rich kid from down the block, and Jimmy, who lived across the street and was always getting yelled at. His mother's voice could curl paint.

"Jim-EEEEE!," she'd yell.

"Don't go," we'd beg.

"I have to," he'd explain.

"Jim-EEEEEEEEEEEE!" she'd scream again.

We were 10 years old and a cross between Peanuts characters and a demon street gang. We'd polarize on various issues, as big groups often do—rich vs. poor, NFL vs. AFL, Democrats vs. Republicans. We'd build tree forts from scrap wood we'd borrow from construction sites down the block. We learned right off that you couldn't use wet composition board for flooring. "Whoops, there goes Joe again." On wet days, we'd lose him two or three times.

We'd declare war on other forts for some manufactured injustice, something that never would've held up in the United Nations. We'd pelt them with crab apples when they least expected it. Then the other fort would counterattack. If you think war doesn't ride in the male bloodstream, just watch a bunch of preadolescent boys at play. For most of us, tree forts were our first exposure to politics and fury.

At night we'd chase lightning bugs and tell myths about the bats that would swoop down to chase mosquitoes. If we played a card game, it was on the porch, surrounded by cans of A&W Root Beer. Whoever drew the ace of spades was doomed to die. And very soon.

If we got enough kids together, we'd play kick the can, to this day the best team sport ever invented. What we'd do is put an old Folger's can in the middle of the driveway and designate one person "it." When he spotted someone lurking in the shadows, he'd call their name and the person would be captured and have to come sit near the can. But if one of players who hadn't been caught was able to run and kick the can, everybody scattered and the game started again. One game lasted 4 days, a record.

As we got a little older, we kept an old torn *Playboy* magazine under a rock near the side of a house. You know, just for reference. It was the most tattered publication since the Declaration of Independence, and, no doubt, one of the most scrutinized. It was full of women the likes of whom we'd never seen before, not only gorgeous but happy to have their clothes off. In fact, the women looked like they'd never been clothed at all, naked since birth. We'd spend long hours arguing about pubic hair and nipples and how old the women might've been. We'd speak authoritatively on where you'd find such creatures. Nobody knew, really. But we all had our theories. California, was one theory. Memphis, another.

On junk day—that glorious time each season when residents could discard water heaters and sewing machines, lawnmowers and beds—we'd ride around on our banana-seat bikes and find things that we could repair.

It was amazing what people would put out on their curbs. Books. Boots. Old pipe. Engines. To this day, I've never understood why someone would throw out an old lawnmower, because they can always be repaired. Always. At the least, you can make a go-cart or a mini-bike from the oily motor.

Jim and Joe's house was the mini-bike capital of the world. Their father, a machinist for Quaker Oats, could make anything out of anything. You'd take him a 3-horsepower Briggs & Stratton lawnmower engine, and he could build you a Maserati or a powerboat. Their older brother Dave would help. It was there, breathing hard over bad engines, that we really learned how to cuss.

When the neighborhood closed in on us, we'd escape on 3-mile rides on our bicycles, with the sole purpose of buying a McDonald's hamburger and fries. Then we'd wash ourselves in the community pool and hurry off to buy Popsicles that would melt and stain our elbows orange.

From all this activity, we ticked like a Timex watch and had the metabolism of a sparrow. Boy, could we eat. We'd guzzle three bottles of Mountain Dew and scarf miles of red licorice. Hot dogs were a favorite. We'd build a fire and spike them with sticks. Chase them with pounds of blackened marshmallows.

To keep in shape, we'd hike to places you could fish for catfish or carp, two underrated game fish. We'd blow crawfish to bits with Black Cat firecrackers someone bought during a summer road trip to Tennessee. There was glory in fireworks. Power in the end of a match.

In winter, we'd sled or skate for hours. At the back of the cemetery, there was this hill that led down to a cul-de-sac. Toboggan runs could go several hundred yards. When the village snow plow cleared the cul-de-sac, it would leave huge piles of snow that we'd fashion into jumps. Ye-Haaaaaaa! Jumps.

Basketball was a winter sport, played on driveways of ice and snow. In summer we'd play football, in helmets and shoulder pads, on 99-degree days. Some sports knew no season other than what struck our fancy at the time. We'd play hockey in July. Pretend to play Augusta in December. We'd invent games that combined the best elements of baseball, dodge-ball, poker, and golf.

This all happened out of doors—a big, rollicking, suburban playground of bugs, snakes, creeks, critters, grass stains, camp fires, splinters, skinned knees, and warm breezes.

And, as it turns out now, certainly no place for kids.

19

AND THEN IT WAS GONE

THERE IS A cookie on the counter. I'm saving it for later, savoring the thought of it. The cookie is one of those big gooey chocolate chip mothers, big as a roasting plate. It resides in a plastic container, the last cookie in sight.

I pass it several times on my way to get coffee or answer the phone, and there it sits tempting me. It couldn't be more appealing, this cookie, if it had cleavage. It licks its lips. Smiles a little. Stronger than most men, I ignore the temptation. As every ad man knows, anticipation is a powerful commodity. Anticipation is what propels us onward.

So I'm saving this cookie for later. I'll have it with a big glass of very cold milk while I watch reruns of *Seinfeld* and laugh at the same old jokes I laughed at last week. The cookie will taste great then. My reward for surviving another day in this house crammed with kids.

There is a $20 in my wallet. How it got there, I don't know. It's been there a while, 90 minutes maybe, which may be a record for a $20 staying in my wallet. They come, and they go. My old leather wallet—my late father's, actually—is the Ellis Island of money.

I think about what I might do with this money later. It's rare for me to have a spare $20 all to myself. I'm usually dishing them out for Friday night school dances, field trips, or birthday gifts. The birthday party cycle in the average American suburb is an economy all its own. One day a year, you get a gift. The other 364 days you are giving them away. That's one of the ways suburbs will nickel and dime you to death.

I consider taking the $20 out to lunch, to the sandwich place on the corner. Or maybe to the teriyaki place a mile away. Every man has his heroin, and teriyaki is mine. I could mainline it daily and still not get enough.

No, on further reflection, I think I will let this $20 stay here a while. Feels right to have a little money in my pocket for once. Later, maybe the wife and I will catch a matinee.

There is a car in the garage. Not a Ferrari. Not a Porsche. No, this is much better than that, a Honda Odyssey, 100,000 miles behind it.

It is only 5, but in car years that's about 50. Needs tires and a front-end alignment. Needs an oil change and probably a new air filter. The car is not complaining. I wash it by hand about every other weekend. Rub it dry. It is the driveway equivalent of heavy-petting. It seems content with that.

The luggage rack is fading, and the remote antitheft device no longer works. I would be more fearful for it, were it not so darned plain. It has all the sex appeal of a wheelchair and the loosey-goosey handling of a supermarket buggy. I like that it's there in the garage. It reminds me of the places we've been, the places we'll never forget. All the places we still have to go.

There is a tulip in the garden. We planted it last fall. First, we went online and ordered the bulb. Then we paid for it with our credit card. Those 2 hours at the computer saved us nearly 2 bucks.

We planted it out front by the mailbox. First impressions, you know? Spring rains nearly drowned it, but the little bulb survived. When the March sun warmed the ground, the little tulip sprang to life. Against all odds, it squirmed through the hard compacted soil, wiggled its way toward the heat above. One April day, its flower opened. Bees buzzed around it like proud fathers. Red with a tan interior, it is clearly the prettiest flower on the street.

In the bedroom, there's a child. He awakens slowly, like a prize fighter from the canvas. He throws an elbow across his face and moans about the agony of waking up. He is up, though, and that is what counts. Eager for the opportunities a new day brings.

From that point, everything that happens is mostly a blur. The teenager enters the kitchen and swipes the cookie. He borrows my last 20 bucks for gas. He climbs in the car, the most dependable I have ever owned, and revs it down the driveway before it has even warmed up. Then, turning sharply and a little too soon, he flattens the little tulip dead.

It was a pretty tulip, but there'll be others. A nice cookie, but we'll bake more. The car was really just any car. And the $20? Who cares?

As he went out the door, he mumbled, "Thanks Dad, see ya later." In a few years, he'll be gone for good. Or for bad. Either way, he'll be gone, and I'll miss the guy more profoundly than I can ever say.

Till then, and without those other replaceable things, I'll manage to cope. Because there's a piece of cake in the refrigerator. A $5-er by the phone . . .

20

NEW STUFF, WILL IT EVER END?

THE TROUBLE with sushi is that I need to eat 7 or 8 pounds of it before I feel like I've had anything at all. I also digest it completely almost immediately after swallowing. So, in many ways, this otherwise light, affordable food winds up being the most expensive meal available.

Strange stuff, sushi. It's merely the ocean's leftovers, made up of items nothing else would eat. Sort of the hot dogs of the sea. Now it's a popular mainstream cuisine. Eventually, we'll make a popular cuisine of the junk we find floating in outer space.

"Yuck," I'll say, the first time I try it.

"When it's prepared properly, you'll love it," some hipster friend will explain.

"Yeah, when it's wrapped in prime rib," I'll say.

Like a lot of guys, I am hugely suspicious and ready to dislike anything that is all the rage. Shirts with big collars. Odd haircuts. Nelly albums. Even cell phones. Since I am incapable of dialing a cell phone without leaving my lane, I assume other drivers are dangerous with them also and that cell phones should be banned from highway use. This is not such a wild assumption. Even with two hands on the wheel, many of today's drivers seem incapable of holding their lanes.

I also find that as cell phones get increasingly smaller, they are even harder to use. The punch pads are too small for the male hand. Like glowing pieces of little purple jewelry. Corrupted by our need to look cool.

The best cell phone we ever had was an old analogue model roughly the size of a carton of milk. We accidentally ran over it several times with the car—cell phones were new back then and we didn't know their limitations—and the thing still worked. As smaller and more fashionable phones came along, with rings that sounded like the orgasms of angels,

my wife tried to destroy this old analog phone. It was a military-like gad-
get, ugly and impossible to break. I think one day, she finally pulled out a
gun and shot it. It didn't make a difference. In fact, I think it worked even
better.

"Bravo company, this is General MacArthur," I used to bark into the
big phone, a war reference that only I would get. So I kept doing it till
people laughed. Like the army itself, I've found that you can pound people
into submission if you're tireless enough.

"Why's Dad keep saying that?" the little girl would ask.

"Because he's a dad," her mother would explain.

"Bravo Company, have you seen my slippers?" I'd ask. "Bravo Company, this is an emergency. Come in."

When we finally decided to trade in the huge, outdated cell phone, it
was like taking an injured pet to the clinic to have it put down. By then,
we'd grown attached to the ridiculous thing. It had become a part of our
household. Strangers would marvel at how unique it was. The kids' friends
would gasp and go, "What's *that*?" It was past its prime but never useless.
In a pinch while camping, I could always use it to pound in a tent stake.

"Do you have your old phone?" the clerk at the cell phone store asked
when we finally went to buy a new one.

"Yes," I said and handed it to him gently. It took two hands to lift,
and you'd always find yourself cradling it so your forearms would do most
of the work.

"By God, look at that!" the clerk gasped when he saw it.

We've had several phones since, none worth remembering. They
seem to shatter easily and get lost in the couch or in shirt pockets. One
night at a movie, I think I accidentally ate one.

Eventually, cell phones will become so miniaturized that they will be
embedded in chips in our teeth and ears. We'll walk around like a nation
of schizophrenics, calling out the phone numbers we want to call, and
then walking down the sidewalk jabbering to someone walking down a
sidewalk 1,000 miles away. Actual human interaction will no longer be
necessary. We can broadcast our snores and our sneezes, our breath mints
and our kisses. Even our very thoughts.

Me, I can't wait.

Computers are another new thing I love. They are to productivity what interstates are to travel—merely faster and not necessarily better. In the long run, computers may not even be faster. A computer lulls you into thinking you are making great progress on some document or report. You'll cut and paste. You'll scan visuals and import them into your document. At 1 o'clock in the morning, in a fit of obsession, you'll include a little bar chart. You will convince yourself that you're the next George Jetson—till you try to print the damn thing out.

Because in my experience 99 percent of all computer problems are printer related. You will spend weeks assembling your project, and then place it at the mercy of some $79 printer with the build quality of a house of toothpicks. When you click on "Print," it will shudder, and then produce half-letters in a language you've never seen before. Then it will jam. After you clear the jam—leaving little bits of shredded paper in its innards—the ink cartridge will run dry. A new print cartridge will require a loan from your local bank, since the cartridges cost more than the printer itself. For years, we've had it all backward: It's the printers that are disposable.

I no longer really know how many phone lines we have coming into the house. Or how many cell phones we own. Or what we spend on AOL accounts. Or cable. I am astounded at the information these gadgets can bring and the research they can do in mere seconds. Occasionally, they seem like good investments. But I am leery of their collective costs, to my pocketbook and my quality of life.

I definitely don't like reading on a computer screen. I prefer the tactile feel of a book or a sports section. I like the feel of a wood product over plastic. And there is something akin to jet lag that sets in after 5 or 6 hours at a computer. Call it e-lag.

At work, I keep a baseball at my desk just to touch something that feels real. I grind the leather baseball in my palms, the way a pitcher does. I practice my curve-ball grip. I zip the ball at bothersome co-workers. When I start my own computer company, for real people with actual sensibilities, each machine will be made of cowhide. The tracking ball will be a Major League baseball.

To this day, some writers shun the computer and prefer to pound a typewriter. I wonder if somehow a writer's initial output on a typewriter isn't a level above what someone would produce with a computer. Does a slower process lead to more deliberate work habits, and hence more thoughtful work? Indeed, it may be the difference between a cabinet maker and a house framer.

Me, I write on an old Mac, and, occasionally, a legal pad. My printer, by the way, has been broken for a month. I don't know what ails it, other than the dialog box that tells me the computer is having trouble connecting/finding the printer. I twisted the cables for 2 hours one morning, sure that they must've worked themselves loose. I rebooted. I prayed.

Nothing.

My next step is to replace the printer cable. Like all good troubleshooters, I go from the easy solution to the more difficult. If the cable replacement doesn't work, I'm out of ideas. And also out of prayers.

I'll probably just go soothe myself with a nice tray of sushi. To my surprise, I'm really starting to like the stuff.

21

MEMOIRS OF
A ROAD TRIP WARRIOR

AMONG MY many fine traits is a humongous bladder, which allows me to drive many hours between bathroom breaks. For us, the great journey seems to be genetically predestined. The way the Nordics were built for the rigors of sea life, we were built for road trips.

But we have our moments.

Once, after a full day in the car with kids, I checked into the motel, came back to the car, checked that everything was okay under the hood, and carried the suitcases to the room, all before realizing that there was a lollipop stuck to the zipper of my shorts. I think it was cherry, though it might've been lime.

Amazingly, no one I ran into mentioned that there was a sucker stuck to my crotch. No one paused to say, "Hey, sir, we usually eat those with our mouths." But I'm sure a dozen people must've seen me, with candy sweetly soldered to the zipper like some sort of hood ornament. I now check for lollipops every time we stop.

Yes, we are veterans of the American highway. Our family has probably taken two dozen major road trips over the course of 20 years. Other families fly—and we do, too, occasionally—but I prefer the open road where you're not so much at the mercy of strangers and airlines that have overbooked your flight. In a car, you go at your own pace. No one asks you to remove your shoes, though we often do anyway.

Traveling by car gives you the chance to pause and appreciate the real America. We once caught a demolition derby on a Saturday night in a small Utah town. From high granite bluffs, we saw paddle wheelers ply the Mississippi River and have paused to watch lightning dance across the Continental Divide.

When the kids were very young and there were a mere two of them, we often traveled between our then–New Orleans home and the grand-parents' place near Chicago. We'd marvel at the kudzu vines in Missis-sippi and the rolling pitch of southern Illinois. It was a 2-day trip. We'd stop overnight in Arkansas, where I'd show the kids how to make paper airplanes from motel room stationery. In a pinch—while waiting for a doctor or a table—a paper airplane is every father's best friend.

The kids were easy then. I could read from the Gideon's Bible, and they would listen closely, wondering when a fairy godmother or a sorcerer would show up. "How can goodness be a partner with wickedness?" I'd read from Corinthians. "How can light live with darkness?"

And they'd be asleep.

I remember as a kid seeing a Bible in a motel room drawer, near the phone, on the table between the beds. My own parents were anemic church-goers, which is to say they rarely went at all. Lapsed Lutherans, they would attend only the occasional Christmas Eve service, when the whole lot of them—aunts, uncles, grandparents—would wander into the big sanctuary with a couple of belts under their belts. Happy and loud, they looked more like people headed to a Dean Martin roast.

I never understood why we didn't attend church more, for these Christmas Eve services in the quiet suburbs of Chicago were almost mythic. It always snowed on the way. Inside, candles were everywhere. Ribbons and greenery adorned the walls. Everyone seemed in a cheery mood, except the Lutheran pastor who screamed at the congregation as if we'd keyed his Plymouth. Evidently, the Lutherans of suburban Chicago required a good scolding every Christmas Eve before returning home and opening too many gifts. In time, I learned that he didn't scold people just on Christmas Eve, but every Sunday.

"Why don't we go to church, Dad?" I once asked.

"Your father thinks the pastor yells too much," my mother would explain, as Dad sat by reading Mike Royko.

Needless to say, Bibles weren't exactly lying around our house, begging to be read. So they became a novelty on the road trips of our youth and continue to catch my eye even today. To me, it's like spotting a family farm or one of those old-timey drive-ins with the trays that attach to the car window. Bibles in the room connect today's adventures to the trips of yesteryear, even as the little laminated card on the TV advertises all the adult channels now available.

When our own kids were very young, they were excited by the prospect of a long car trip to see the grandparents. Back then, you could tell small innocent fibs that they would never figure out. "Keep an eye out for deer," you'd say, and they would spend 2 hours peering out at the interstate, waiting for Bambi to come jogging along the I-55. "If you're good, we'll get pizza," you'd say about 4 p.m., the witching hour for any long car trip.

Because, as good as kids are, no kid is good in a car between the hours of 4 and 6 p.m., after having spent 8 hours on the road. You could promise them lobster, cash, or a rare first-reading of the family will, and there would be no placating them. They would squeal like cats in a canary cage.

On trips like that, you look in the back at 4:30, and all you see are feet in the air. No socks. Their toes are painted in blue or orange Magic Marker. You can be sure they're inserting something inappropriate into their belly buttons: pennies laced with Krazy Glue.

By 5, they are searching under the seats for stray fries from yesterday's lunch. One will be sucking on a dirty sock. They will be naked from the waist up and hanging their T-shirts out the window, trying to flag down passing truckers. "We've been in this car for 9 hours!" they'd plead to the truckers, faces all scrunched. The truckers would merely look down and wave pleasantly.

By 5:30, the kids will have broken apart the Etch A Sketch and fashioned the pieces into a small handgun. They plan their mutiny carefully. One will hold the Etch A Sketch handgun, and the other will take the wheel from the old guy. Someone else will pounce on his bossy girlfriend. It's a daring move, but they are desperate. For almost 10 hours, they have been smelling their dad, and frankly he doesn't smell so hot—like dress shirts after their mother irons them too long. Plus, he's got that humongous bladder. It appears now that, unless forced, he will never stop. At 6, just as the mutiny is about to begin, he pulls into the motel.

This is an exciting moment, when he pulls into the motel. Is the pool nice? Where are the soda machines? Does the motel have indoor-outdoor carpet along the walkways? This is almost always a bad sign for a motel. Any sign of Astroturf means that the motel is probably some ma and pa operation, and there will be lots of noisy, dripping air conditioners. Even when young, the kids could see the advantages that a good Holiday Inn offered. It featured dashing, dynamic children much like themselves. The air-conditioning was invisible—or at least not drippy. Vending machines offered brand-name nuts.

❦

Our road trips became more complicated as the kids became older and more numerous. To make it less boring, we'd buy them books and video games. They would tire of them after 20 minutes and then begin to question the wisdom of such an adventure. They'd cast doubt about whether we were headed in the right direction and whether this was the best time of year to be going. Would there be dry road in the Rockies? Could we clear Donner Pass?

They'd talk about all the wonderful trips their friends' families were taking, exotic trips to Hawaii or France. It wasn't meant as criticism. No, not at all. They were just filling us in on what some of the others were up to.

"And then they're going to New Zealand," one would say.

"Where's that?"

"Near Old Zealand," another would answer.

By the time we'd reached Barstow, the dialogue was mostly along these lines, delivered with squinty cowboy glares.

Boy to older sister: You shut up.

Older sister to boy: You shut up.

Little girl to boy: Why are you so mean?

Boy to younger sister: You shut up.

Mother: Okay, everybody please be quiet and play with your new games.

Boy: I don't even like these games.

Older daughter: You picked them out.

Boy to older daughter: You shut up.

Older sister to boy: You shut up.

You get the idea. Variations of this would go on for hours. Sometimes, I would pull to the rest stop and threaten them physically. It's not the worst thing for a dad to pop his top now and then. It sets limits to childish behavior and exorcises murderous thoughts.

For 2,000 miles we'd bond like this. They would act up. Then their mother would intercede and make them promises we could never keep.

"If you finish that book, I'll buy you a McDonald's," she'd say.

"Which McDonald's?" they'd ask.

"Any one you'd like."

"I hate McDonald's," the older daughter would say.

"Me too," I'd say.

"Okay, I'll buy you something else," their mother would say.

"What?"

"A Kennedy," she'd say. "I'll buy you your own Kennedy."

"They're for sale?" the older daughter would ask.

To a certain extent, everybody is. Everybody has their price. On this day, in the stuffy car, the notion that you could buy or sell people is an interesting notion for them. We go 50 miles with hardly a fistfight.

"Honestly, I'd rather have one of the Nixon girls," I'd tell my wife.

"Who are the Nixon girls?" someone would ask.

It'd explain to them about Julie and Tricia and how they always looked dressed for Easter and had hair that resembled bakery confections. It was a nice look back then, and even if you didn't like their dad, you couldn't help but have a certain thirst for his Barbie doll daughters.

"That's too much information," their mother would say.

"Keep going, Dad," said the boy, his voice mysteriously lower.

I could do a decent 45 minutes on the Nixons. I'd tell the kids about the Checkers speech—they prefer any story with a dog—and how Nixon once promised that the press wouldn't have him to kick around anymore, when in fact he would later return to make a very disgraceful exit. It was, I explained, almost classic literature.

"Like King Richard," chimed in their mother.

"Who's he?" the boy would ask.

"Jeeeesh," his sister would whoosh, one of those steam-whistle sounds that comes out of a kid's mouth.

"Shut up," the boy would say.

"You shut up," the older daughter would answer.

We once got into a shouting match while stopped along a pristine stretch of the Colorado River, west of Denver. Who remembers the cause. Even then, I'm sure it was unclear. Someone probably made an unkind remark about someone's Band-Aid. It escalated, and someone was threatening not to get in the car again with the offending party.

"Great, one less for dinner," I said and started the car.

By the time we pulled away, they were always all back in the car, clicking their seatbelts in, staring out the window with the dreary expressions of prisoners whose parole is so far down the pike, they don't even look at a calendar.

Of course, once we got there, they loved the Midwest. On trips to see the grandparents, they'd chase fireflies and ice cream trucks. They turned the garden hose on each other on hot days and spent long afternoons on the Chicago lakefront, eating brats and Chicago-style dogs, by far the best dogs anywhere. We would take them into the city, and by the time they had dogs for lunch and deep-dish pizza for dinner, they'd have gained 15 pounds each and begun to waddle. The Midwest has more waddlers than California. In California, the general populace tends to be thinner, more nervous, and, strangely, not quite so happy. There's no doubting the role good greasy meat plays in day-to-day satisfaction.

We soon developed a routine for our car trips. I spent the day or two before scrubbing the car as if it were about to be married. My wife would visit the car club and bring home volumes of information on our destination. Year it was founded. Motel options. Where to rent a horse. Those sorts of things.

I'd give the kids a pep talk beginning about a week before, saying things like "You know, the Cubs are in town," or, "I know a great little place to catch sunfish."

"Really, Dad?"

"Really."

"You're kidding?"

"I'd never kid a kid," I explained.

A sunfish is a great game fish. It's about the size of a potato chip and much harder to eat. But they'd get excited anyway. The boy would rush to the basement to find our vintage 1964 fishing tackle. The monofiliment crumbled in your fist as you tried to string the rod. We'd make trips to the sporting goods store—there is no place more exciting before a summer vacation—and ask which fishing line they might recommend.

"What'll you be catching?" the clerk would ask.

"Heat stroke, probably," I say.

"My dad, he just likes to sit in the boat," the boy explained.

Sure enough, there is nothing wrong with sitting in a boat and watching the way the dragonflies drift upon a pond. I have nothing against a bass grabbing the lure and high-tailing it for the other side of the lake. But fish are the debutantes of the great outdoors, feeding at the most ungodly hours—early morning or late at night. I prefer to pursue fish that eat when I do. The sunfish is one. Catfish are another.

So we assembled all our fishing gear, purchased a few new lures, and stock the tackle box with fresh and shiny hooks.

"Should we take this net?" the boy asked.

"Is it big enough?" I'd reply.

"Let's take it, Dad," he'd say.

"Okay."

We fish in hopes of coming home with a few stories, that is all. One evening, near Lake Tahoe, we walked a nearby river in the early evening in hopes of convincing a rainbow trout to sample the salmon eggs we offered on a number 14 hook, barely the size of an eyelash. Even though we'd used bug spray, the mosquitoes were horrific. It got darker and darker and quieter and quieter. Once in a while, a car whooshed by on the road 100 yards away, but other than that all we heard were the sounds of us slapping at the mosquitoes. The bushes were thick along the river's edge, so we pushed our way through to the water.

For 20 minutes, we fished without success, though we could occasionally see a fish break water. At one point, something just down river from us—20 to 30 yards—decided to go in after the fish. We never saw it, just heard the splash of something big taking to the Truckee River.

"Dad?"

"Yeah?"

"What was that?"

I couldn't imagine. From the size of the splash, I suspected a bear. We didn't stay around to find out.

"What *was* that?" we kept asking each other on the way home.

"Big Foot," I said, and I wasn't really joking.

As the kids evolved, so did our car trips. When there were four of them, we'd often take two vehicles, and if there's ever inspiration for a father to hurry on down the highway, it's the sight of a teenage daughter in a rear-view mirror, holding the wheel with her elbows while plucking her eyebrows.

"Should she be doing that?" I'd ask her mother by cell phone.

"Doing what?"

"Plucking while she drives?" I'd ask.

"Don't worry, I'm holding the wheel," my wife would say.

That didn't always free me of worry, that the car going 70 mph right behind us was being steered by a woman in the passenger seat while the driver plucked away. I'd usually insist that my older daughter wait till we reached our destination to engage in such activities. She'd pull three more hairs and stop immediately.

With two cars, the boys could be in one car; the girls in another. To this day, I'm amazed at how easily things break down along gender lines.

"Dad, don't let them pass," the boy might say.

"I like it better," I'd tell him, "when those pluckers are in front of us."

Our favorite trips now are from Los Angeles to Lake Tahoe, a lake that remains a deep, mountain blue. It seems to sparkle at all times, a boater's lake with little coves surrounded by snow-capped peaks.

From LA, it takes us about 8 hours to reach it by car, a length of time acceptable to young temperaments tuned to a world dependent on microwaves and call-waiting.

In two vehicles, they squabble only half as much. In fact, they seem to enjoy these short stints up into the mountains more than they would any plane ride or cruise ship. The girls like the fact that they don't have to listen to the boys' music. We like the fact that no one in our vehicle will discuss Brad Pitt's calf muscles or the proper way to marry rich.

These trips have changed in other ways as well. There is no indoor-outdoor carpet in the vacation houses that we rent. No Bibles in the drawers. No lollipops on my crotch. Just expensive corkscrews and directions on how to work the trash compactor.

It's a spiritual trade off: corkscrews for Bibles. If it were up to me, I'd have them both. In the drawer by the bed. Up by the perfect mountain lake, half a mile from heaven.

22

THE THOUGHTS
CHRISTMAS BRINGS

Dear Santa,

Sorry about the cookies. The kids set them out for you, and then couldn't resist taking a bite. Willpower was never a strong suit for them. Nor for me. I drank your eggnog.

It is nearly midnight, and I noticed they didn't leave you a note of gratitude. Let me assure you that was not how they were raised. Our kids were raised to say please and thank you, to hold doors for old ladies, and to clean up picnic sites before they left. So far, I'm guessing they're batting about .471. Is that better than most kids? You'd know better than I.

I hope your evening is going well. I hope you didn't encounter anti-aircraft fire over the Middle East or bad weather over Buffalo. Flying is such a bitch these days. Can I talk like that to Santa? Pardon me, but there's no better word.

I hope we can talk frankly here, on Christmas Eve, the most profound and spiritual night of the year. There's something in the stars tonight, isn't there? Something that suggests some bigger truth.

Charles Lindbergh—like you, a renowned long-distance flyer—once noted that we talk least about the things we think about the most. I find that to be true. The only thing I can't figure out is exactly what other guys are thinking about. Their credit? Their cars? I know what I'm thinking about: my job, my wife, my kids, my fear of screwing it all up. I know most other guys think about their wives and their kids. Do they ever think about screwing up? Do they ever worry about not being able to take care of everyone they take care of, while fantasizing about the pony-tailed young waitress who just dropped the cheeseburger on the table in front of them? Was that flirtation or a friendly smile? Do I look closer to 40 or 80? How about these pants? Good? How healthy's my heart?

These are the sort of things I dwell on. Do you? Probably not. You seem too well adjusted—a very good businessman with a large charitable streak. You're too busy for self-doubt or philosophy. Is that normal? Or is that just a front?

I always wonder, at what point do we cross the line from self-examination to self-absorption? Is this something you think about while you're trying to fill the sleigh? Do you ever think back on the things you didn't do, the risks you didn't take? In hindsight, you probably should've trademarked Rudolph, right? You probably could've sold oil rights to the North Pole.

You're very old school, Santa. Yet, you still manage to compete.

As you well know, midlife is a very weird area code. I'm thinking I like it mostly. It seems to suit my soul, which was never particularly jocular or carefree. Yet, at middle age, I've seen enough to worry over how quickly it all passes: the lush summers, the beautiful falls, the holiday parties. With kids, especially, the clock ticks too quickly. Their years seem defined by the school year, which is only 9 months long. They seem to go from kindergarten to third grade in a heartbeat. From fifth grade to high school at the speed of light. Pretty soon, they'd rather talk to their friends than to you. How do you not take this personally, when your own flesh and blood prefers the company of somebody named Kaylene or Courtney, ghostlike figures in low-cut jeans who whisk through the house as if on mopeds, smiling but not pausing to say hello. I don't take this personally, of course. Do you?

I know these are a lot of innermost thoughts for one little Santa note. I know men aren't supposed to talk like this. But it's the holidays, and the Christmas brandy is getting to me a little. Got another minute? Great. Here, let me pour you a glass.

You know, it seems to me we go through three phases in our lives. When we are young, we try to please out parents. As adults, we try to please our spouses and our bosses. But it's not till we turn 45 or 50—till we really grow up—that we realize we have to some day please ourselves. What a selfish, indulgent thought, that we deserve to be a little happy. But if we don't look out for ourselves, who will, right? Am I way off the mark here? Or are these merely the jagged ramblings of a father who overspent at Target? Probably a little of both.

Well, that's all for now. You probably have things to do. I have a tricycle to try to put together. While the others sleep, I will tend to the toys and try to find that bracelet I bought my wife last night. Hey, you're the pro: What do you get for someone you've known 100 years? Is cash okay, or do they prefer something with more growth potential, say T-bills or municipal bonds? A T-bill doesn't seem very romantic, but it's a tough time for romantics. Love seems a fading art form.

You know, maybe I should just write my wife a very nice note. That's what I'll do: tell her how much she means to me and how I never say that often enough. How I admire her strength and her humor and the way she still looks great in those white cotton pants. Nothing too pornographic, of course, just the basics about what a fine tush she has. And how I still catch myself leering.

For it's Christmas, after all, and if you can't tell the truth on Christmas, what's the point? Truth is God's gift, and having someone to be truthful with is probably even a greater reward: a friend, a lover, a Santa, a saint. With her, I've got all four. As my old man used to say: Who'd-a-thunk-it, huh?

Well, pal, thanks for listening. Sorry the house is such a mess. It's been crazy here, to say the least. I swear, next year we're getting rid of that ratty old couch. Next December 24th, you'll hardly recognize the place, save for the handprints on the wall and the nose prints on the windows.

Till then, be well, my friend. Oh, and Merry Christmas. As they used to say in Bethlehem, don't be a stranger.

23

NOTORIOUS D.A.D.

THAT'S MY rapper name. Notorious D.A.D. I use it in my role as cultural watchdog and protector of innocent young lives. I haven't figured out what it stands for yet. Just be warned that I am very serious about it. As I am about most things.

When I remind my wife of this, and that my name is now Notorious, she doesn't hesitate in her work. I am holding the baby, who has developed a fondness for grabbing fistfuls of my T-shirt in a gesture of rapper solidarity. When the baby does this, he inadvertently grabs a wad of my notoriously sensitive chest hair, forcing me to cry out in anguish.

"Yeeeeeowwww," I say.

"What's wrong now, Notorious?" my wife asks.

"He keeps grabbing my chest hair," I explain, sometimes through tears.

Thus ensues a 20-minute discussion over whether I should get my chest waxed. Her point is that every man gets his chest waxed these days. My point is how do you know that, exactly?

"I just know," she says.

I contemplate a society where all men get their chests waxed, and I decide I don't want to live in such a world. I am who I am. Notorious. Stubborn. And hairy as a goat.

"I'll bet Eugene gets his chest waxed," she notes.

No doubt. Eugene's a vegetarian. Obviously, there are no limits to what he'll do to his body. There's a tattoo on his ankle. Has a haircut like Sting. He's a TV producer, for god's sakes.

"Bad example," I say.

"What about Irv?" she asks.

Irv? I've seen Irv at the beach. He looks like he's wearing puppies on his chest. He's so hairy that when he's naked, it's like he's still fully clothed. I don't think Irv's skin has ever felt the sun, or the cold breath of autumn. Even when he goes into the ocean, he doesn't really get wet. He couldn't be any drier if he wore a wet suit.

"Irv?" I say.

"Okay, not Irv," says my wife. "But I'll bet the rest do."

There was a time when a hairy chest was a sign of virility. I'd be hard-pressed to say when that all changed. For I just discovered that "everybody" is getting their chests waxed. Rarely have I felt so alone.

"What are you watching, Dad?" the little girl asks.

"TV," I say.

"But what?" she asks.

"I'm not sure," I say.

I make a special effort to stay atop what is happening in our culture, if only so that at cocktail parties when someone scoffs, "I hate my kid's music; I just hate that crap," I can nod knowingly.

Granted, no generation ever approved of their children's music. It will be sweet revenge indeed to see what our grandchildren will use to drive their parents batty. I will relish every sour note, knowing that I, formerly known as Notorious D.A.D., once endured similar tortures.

We live in a society that worships Eminem even as it adores Dr. Phil, a big, fat, sanctimonious Texan whose downfall I await like Christmas. It is the preachers among us who fall the hardest. Remember William Bennett? Or Jimmy Swaggart? Or even Bill Clinton? Scratch a moralist, and you don't have to go deep before you reveal the hypocrite beneath.

In this world of kooks and criminals, I hope to find a sensible middle ground. Where young musicians can try new things and movies can mine their laughs by pushing the envelope of what's acceptable. It is not an easy task. A recent episode of an animated show on family life included a scene where Geppetto, in a crude attempt at sodomy, was trying to persuade Pinocchio to lie, so that his nose would grow. You'd have to see it to believe it.

Then again, maybe you wouldn't.

Speaking of culture, we went to an actual Hollywood premiere once.

Okay twice, but "once" sounds better and makes it seem more accidental and not so noxious. Believe me, it's not because we're any sort of hotshots in the community. Reside in Los Angeles long enough, and you'll eventually be invited to a premiere. If you can find a sitter, you should go.

I do this willingly, as a dad and cultural watchdog, and as someone who can't resist a free night out. Yet I always have this sense of remorse, an hour before leaving the house, that I'd really rather spend the evening with my kids. Color with my toddler. Talk about Craig Biggio's batting stance with my older son. Just before leaving, I always get a sense of social remorse, that whatever I would be doing at home would be far better than what I'm about to get into outside of it. I am wrong. Occasionally, you just need to get out.

Attending a movie premiere is pretty much just like going to the movies, except the lines are longer and everyone else in the audience makes way more money than you do. Some people arrive in limos, but you probably won't. The 1,000 or so guests are friends and business associates of the stars and producers. They herd you around like sheep. Popcorn is free. If anyone anywhere is able to afford a $4 bag of popcorn, it's a movie industry crowd. But here, it is all on the house.

After the movie is when it gets interesting. Nearby, on the studio lot or in some club, they will throw a party. Famous athletes will be there. Actors and actor wanna-bes. Agents, moguls, mothers, and fathers. Kids will run wild. Caterers will serve ribs, chicken, shrimp, and alcohol in vast quantities. It is, mostly, a prom for 40-year-olds. Not so dressy, surprisingly casual, actually. Jeans and T-shirts and sports jackets. These are the people who entertain America. Honestly, most of them look like your brother-in-law the dentist.

There will be various games you can play. And one thing you can be sure of: Everyone will love—*love!*—the movie they just saw for the first time.

I am like a carp amid lobster at one of these things. The sort of people I usually smirk at are 4 feet away. Maria Shriver. Russell Crowe. Terrell Owens. I sense at any moment, some flunkie will approach and say, "Sir, please come with me." Off to the side, some guy in a blazer and ear-piece will explain that there has been some mistake and that I really wasn't supposed to be invited to this royal fete. My invitation was supposed to go to Tom Wopat or Kristen Davis. "Could we have the badge back, please? This man will escort you out."

Never, in my two premieres, has this happened. But it's bound to. Just the thought of it is enough to keep me home where I belong. Unless, of course, they invite me again. If I can find a sitter, we will go. Did I mention they were free?

Back on the home front, I am watching network TV with the little girl, a program about a fat slob of a husband and a good-looking wife. They have kids who question them at every turn. At first, I think it might be one of those reality shows. Or maybe a video from our last Christmas.

"You like this show?" I ask the little girl.

"No," she says.

"Then why do you watch it?" I ask.

She shrugs.

Having the TV on constantly is like having strangers in the house all the time—an invasion of privacy, an oddball lifestyle. I try to be selective about what we watch and to make them turn the TV off on homework nights. But far too often, the TV is going when there is nothing worthy of our attention. It's just on. Like the furnace.

I switch the channel. As a guy, I am able to deduce in micro-seconds whether a show is worthwhile or not. A snippet of bad dialogue, a laugh track, and even cheesy lighting can alert me to impending disappointment. I don't think women and girls have these same reflexes. They prefer to linger over a show for 5 seconds or so. In 5 seconds, I can cruise a hundred channels, with time left over to make pudding.

"Slow down, Dad," the little girl says.

"This *is* slow," I say, clicking through a dozen shows.

It is odd the things that lure me. A tacky religious show will entertain me for 15 minutes. I always wonder what is going on behind the scenes of such shows, the squabbles over airtime and who'll sing what. The legions of makeup artists and big hair architects. The unplanned pregnancies and the illicit dressing room rendezvous. Okay, so maybe none of that happens. But it's an amusing scenario for these phony-baloney hosts. When you wear your mascara thick as axle grease, you're pretty much capable of anything.

"Dad!" the little girl yells after 5 minutes of this.

"Yes?"

"Change the channel!" she pleads as if possessed.

And on we go to other things: the poker channel, the jewelry testimonials. If I pause at all, I fear the toddler will want to insert another one of those Barney tapes we've watched a thousand times. One more verse of "Wheels on the Bus," and I'm likely to climb to the roof and hurl myself into the bougainvillea. It'll take them a week to find me. They'll see the ladder but no sign of me, Notorious D.A.D., face down in a bush full of thorns. Just another martyr. Believe me, it'd beat another round of Barney.

Or the *Wiggles* show. Have you seen the *Wiggles* show? It's a bunch of grown men dressed in orange and yellow *Star Trek* shirts dancing and acting silly. Naturally, the children love the *Wiggles* and will watch them the way I watch Kentucky Derbies or Super Bowls. They bounce on their little butts—the kids, not the actors—and pretend to move along to the music, which I find impossible to dance to myself. Tried it a couple of times. Believe me, it's hopeless.

"Let's watch this," the little girl says.

"Okay," I say, and we settle in to another show.

This next show is called *Desperate Housewives*, a title I find rather redundant. Of all the housewives I've known, most of them have been desperate, if not downright possessed. It's being around kids that does it.

In this episode, Teri Hatcher, who used to go steady with Superman, is trying to seduce a plumber who lives next door. All the men love Teri. She's sort of the Becky Thatcher of the show, but with more cosmetic surgery, obviously.

Meanwhile, there's that redhead who's trying to poison her doctor husband, which I find implausible, since the doctor is a pretty good guy and anyone who has ever lived in suburbia will tell you that you never poison a pretty good guy—doctor or not. Sure, doctors can be a little imperious and this one apparently was fooling around, but so be it. Redheads, I swear. . . .

Everywhere on this show, women seem to be the aggressors. It's a case of art imitating my house. The underlying theme of *Desperate Housewives* is that women are working at this very moment to dominate the world, using any means at their disposal. Lord help the next generation of young men coming along.

For example, there is a subplot involving the Eva Longoria character, who is testifying in court to try to save her crooked husband—who knows why, since she is having a very satisfying relationship with the youngster who mows her lawn. As a former lawn boy, I know this goes on all the time. It can turn a simple 20-minute lawn job into an hour or more.

There are other things going on here, too. One mother is being forced to go back to work after interfering with her husband's career, a cautionary tale for nearly all of us. There are also whacko teens, lustful blondes, and a narrator back from the grave. I have no idea why this show is so popular. On our little cul-de-sac, stuff like this happens almost hourly.

"Is this appropriate?" my wife asks when she sees the little girl and me watching *Desperate Housewives*.

"It's actually kind of boring," I say.

"But it is appropriate?" she asks again.

I want to explain to her that learning of such behavior helps me to become a better man. But there's that Calvinist buzzword again: appropriate. When a mother uses the work "appropriate," it's best to take her seriously.

It applies to music and school plays, clothing and language. I no longer know what's appropriate for a 12-year-old or a 16-year-old. The yardstick is always moving, the boundaries always pushed. You try to see what other parents allow and gauge yourself there. But mostly, you have to trust your gut, which in my case gets bigger every year. Talk about moving yardsticks.

I am determined to pay attention, no matter what the cost. I'll sit through crude lyrics. Suggestive dialogue. Bad sitcoms, if only to know what my kids are being exposed to. It's all part of a dad's job today.

When I was a kid, the porn movie *Deep Throat* was all the rage. Is there anything today quite as crude?

Notorious D.A.D., cultural watchdog, doesn't think so. But stay tuned. It's not like they're not out there trying.

24

HOMEWORK AND HORMONES

HERE I AM at 6:50 in the morning, writing a note to the school office about my youngest daughter's lip, which she injured in an accident involving the ice cream scoop that became attached to her face while she was watching the toddler a week or so ago. It was sort of amusing at the time, but now her lower lip is chapped and sore, possibly infected. Honestly, do these things ever happen to you?

She needs a note that will get her out of class in time to see the doctor about her swollen, possibly infected, lip. Something short and to the point, which is my weakest area as a writer of school notes. The art of writing a note to the office is to seem authoritative and grateful all at the same time. A tall order, for someone with my literary skills.

As I craft the note, I am feeling uncommon sympathy for the person whose job it is to read these notes all morning long. I'd love to send them something more interesting and true to life. Something that would hold her attention, along the lines of:

To whom it may concern:

Please excuse my daughter Emily from class early today. Her lip may be infected due to a babysitting incident. I won't go into details.

Rest assured that we will return her to school as promptly as possible. It is our belief that you are doing an outstanding job with the sons and daughters of this community. Having met several, I know that you have your work cut out for you.

Me? I'm doing fine, though at work lately I just can't seem to get on track. Maybe it's that extra glass of wine I'm having in the evenings. Okay, so it's more than one. Okay, so it's several.

Or maybe it's that new medication I'm on. I forget its name, but it ends with an x. Do the names of all medications now end with x? This stuff, whatever it is, makes me loopy and prone to long walks late at night. Could you recommend a good internist?

To be honest, my life is not working out so well. I don't know what I had in mind, but I didn't suspect that I would be at the mercy of such idiots. As I get older, I now must grow accustomed to working for people younger than myself. In addition to being idiots, they are younger idiots, which is the worst form of idiocy, trust me. Oh, that's right, you work in a school.

My marriage also seems doomed. I love my wife dearly, but lately she seems listless and unresponsive. During our romantic dinners together, she is often distracted. When I come back from the restroom, I find that she has joined tables of complete strangers. She is not looking for another man. She is looking for a better person. Good luck.

Our community is very nice, but as you know it runs on gossip, money, and innuendo. It is, in fact, like a giant version of the seventh grade, except the kids are far older and occasionally crazy. Some are very rich. Others are just cutting it. There is a subtext of envy and class warfare at all times. We plead with our kids that cars are just cars and houses just houses and that the really important things in life are relationships, friends, and family. In reality, I'm finding that material things count for a whole lot: safety, security, peace of mind. I'm a revisionist materialist. I now crave good things. And a boat.

I hope you understand our dilemma. If you could just release Emily for her doctor's appointment at 12:45, that would go a long way to improving our situation. I am forever in your debt. If you ever need to talk, please let me know.

Gratefully, Emily's dad.

That is the letter I long to send to the attendance office. I think it would clear up a lot of possible misunderstandings that have occurred over the years between school officials and our family. The letter is long and perhaps too detailed. But frankly, it didn't even go into the whole squabble we recently had over homework. My God.

Our daughter is finishing up a massive Civil War report. It is to homework what Hiroshima was to bug control. It is the master's thesis of the eighth grade, a mind-bending 40 pages, with 1-inch margins. Dare go 1.25 on the margins, and you'll be sorry.

"Was Missouri a border state?" my wife asks.

"I'm not sure," says the little girl.

"Look it up," her mother orders.

"I can't now; I have my math," the little girl replies.

"Look it up now," her mother says.

This is not a static conversation. If this were music, the previous exchange would begin below the staff and finish far above it. Word by word, the conversation gets louder and a little more shrill. It is like one of those operas where the butcher dies, and then it is revealed he was having an affair with the town maiden. And the town maiden sings her pretty heart out. That's what this conversation sounds like.

For a week, it's been like this. And I can tell you this about our little house: Homework and hormones do not mix.

"You should really," I say, "let your daughter do this herself."

"She's way behind," her mother says.

"All the other parents are helping, Dad," the little girl explains.

Well, that's where you lose me. I'll help if the printer jams or if I need to run her to the library for a reference book. I'll take her to a drugstore to buy a binder or over to her friend Olivia's house to borrow some notes. But I won't sit at the computer rewriting her Civil War report. I won't. And I don't care what all the other parents do.

"Why was the Battle of Pea Ridge fought?" my wife asks.

Not sure. But I suspect it was over homework.

We live in an increasingly competitive world. The good state schools, the only ones we can afford, have become as selective as the Ivy League. The Ivy League? Who actually gets in there anymore?

So, with perfectly good intentions, parents help more than we should. We fret over the proper preschool and battle with the kindergarten teachers. We challenge the fifth-grade math curriculum and help research the eighth grade Civil War report. When it comes time to go off to college, I'm pretty sure some of these parents will go along.

"Mom, why are you packing?"

"I'm going with you."

"Mom!"

"I hear the French lit class is very tough," the mom will explain.

A newsmagazine recently wrote of a group of mothers who attended their kids' last lunch at high school, just to watch them eat. "Get a life," the kids yelled out. "You are our lives," the mothers answered.

My wife is the most stable, sensible, organized, responsible wife I know. When it comes to common sense—which, frankly, isn't all that common—she puts me to shame. But this is the conversation we just had:

"Know what time I made it to bed last night?" she asks.

"1 a.m.?" I ask.

"4:30," she says.

She was up till 4:30 coloring a U.S. map with crayons. Double-checking the margins. Triple-checking the syntax. Correcting spelling. When this is over, she's going to really know this Civil War.

"When was Lincoln president?" she asks.

"1860 to 1865?" I guess.

"It wasn't 1835," she says.

"That's what she had?"

"Yup, that's what she had."

So here's another note I long to write.

Dear attendance office,

Mrs. Erskine will not be volunteering in the library today on account of she was up until 4:30 a.m. typing her daughter's Civil War report. They panicked when they realized the margins were set at 1.25 instead of the mandatory 1.0. This meant that several chapters were shorter than required and needed to be embellished. While embellishment is a good use of my wife's time, I honestly think it is something my daughter should be doing. For if you're not going to learn to embellish by the eighth grade, when will you ever learn?

My daughter Emily is dragging a little today, too, so if you could keep an eye on her, I would really appreciate it. She was up making her mother coffee and rubbing her shoulders till well after 1 a.m., on the heels of her championship softball game that same evening. When I dropped her at school today, she rolled to the pavement in a heap, and it took me several minutes to revive her. This concerned me, till I realized that many of the children were falling to the ground in heaps as well. Is this common? Should I be more concerned?

I'm finding this to be an increasingly odd and lonely planet. Doesn't it seem that we are putting more and more pressure on children to achieve? Granted, it's a more competitive world, but where does it all end? I wonder what Dickens would say about it all. Twain would have a field day.

In any event, thanks as always for your help and understanding. I hope that this is the last letter I need to write to you this week. In any case, good luck. If you ever need to talk . . .

Gratefully, Emily's dad.

25

MAKE FRIENDS, LIVE FOREVER

FRIENDS ARE good for you. Harvard researchers found that having friends improves the conditions of the arteries and cuts down on something they call "inflammatory markers." Stripper friends don't count. Nor do bartenders or bookies. We're talking buddies here, buddy. According to the Harvard study, the more the merrier.

In real life, I've found that it is better to have one good friend than a lot of mediocre friends. The more friends you have, the more likely it is that one of them will steal your wife, or worse, fail to return any good garden tools they've borrowed over the weekend.

When choosing friends, look for someone like you, only better. The rules of dating apply: Appearance is important, as is a sense of humor or membership to a good country club. They don't necessarily need to be literate, but it never hurts. Maybe they have a fishing boat and are generous with their leisure. You shouldn't appear too eager in pursuing a new friend, for fear of scaring the potential friend away. As in all things, cool counts.

I have, I'm proud to say, several friends. I would recommend none of them. Paul is too needy. Don too successful. If anything is a turnoff to me, it's guys who make way more money than I do. It's not sporting of them and creates barriers to our friendship. Don is all the time picking up the tab. The nerve.

"I got this," I'll say.

"Nope," he'll say, grabbing the dinner bill.

"You got the last one," I'll say.

"I did?" he'll say, knowing full well he did.

What follows is a series of table thumping gestures to try to get the check first, which alarms surrounding diners and makes the waitress uncomfortable. So as not to make a scene, I always give up first.

Pete's a fine and funny friend, too, but his wife is far too pretty, making him ineligible for close friendship. She's a leggy dentist, and I find that in her presence, I constantly regret not having flossed, which she is always on me about. Seeing her also takes me back to that moment in college when I realized that there were some girls who were clearly out of reach. The tall ones, mostly, but almost all of the Delta Gammas, who breezed across campus as if their butts were jet engines. In winter, they huddled together against the cold, even though they wore expensive, fur-lined jackets. In spring, they drove convertibles that were nicer than anything the professors drove. They came back tan from spring break, kissed by the sun and whomever else they pleased.

The point is, it's difficult to have a friend whose wife is spectacular and redolent of so many things. I prefer friends with merely good-looking wives. It's easier on the nerves.

Jack is a good friend. As is Chris. Irv? One of the best. All are different. All special in their own special ways.

For many men, imaginary friends work best. Like Jimmy Stewart had in *Harvey*. You can create imaginary friends yourself, taking the best characteristics of all your friends and blending them into one person. Think of it as a friendship buffet. Here's my imaginary friend.

- Has season tickets to the Lakers.
- Always has an extra Cuban cigar.
- Looks remarkably like Denise Richards.
- Owns a bass boat.
- Does a great Bill Murray impression.
- Doesn't mind helping when a pipe bursts.

In the suburbs, a pipe is always bursting. At some point, the water main will go. This is the big pipe that runs from the street to the house and supplies the millions and millions of gallons a family needs each day. Repairing it almost always means tearing up the yard and going a day or two without flushing. Try not to go all to pieces. It's just a water main.

As a rule, water mains only explode on Sundays or on the eve of some big party, requiring a husband to step up and take emergency measures.

But it is then that you'll know who your friends are. Bruce will be out of town. Tom will be at a ball game. Thank God for imaginary friends.

"Hey, what happened to the yard?" your wife will ask.

"Water main exploded," you'll say.

"OH MY GOD!" she'll scream. "OH MY GOD OF GODS!"

"Don't worry, it's just a water main," you'll tell her calmly.

"Nice pond," a neighbor will call over, as water begins to fill the yard and seep under the front door.

"Thanks," you'll say.

Never fear. Your imaginary friend will be standing by holding a pipe wrench. In my case, she has a white T-shirt tied around her slender waist and a hand on her hip. She is so thin, you can identify all her ribs and, perhaps, her gallbladder. I'll rub my eyes, marveling at such a wonderful vision. For, on her fingers, are all the different pipe fittings a guy could ever want.

"Half-inch elbow?" she offers.

"Of course," I say.

"Or, three-quarter-inch copper union?" she'll purr.

"Both?" you'll say, voice rising sharply.

Sometimes a pipe fitting is just a pipe fitting. Other times, well . . .

"Here, let me take that shovel," the imaginary friend says.

"No, I insist," I'll say.

"Okay, we'll dig together," she says.

Working closely, my imaginary friend and I dig a trench in which to lay the new pipe. It takes us several hours, so I am forced to keep applying sunscreen to her neck and shoulders.

"You have nice hands," she'll say.

"I like your vertebrae," you'll answer.

"How much longer?" yells someone from the kitchen.

"Who's that?" my imaginary friend will ask.

"My conscience," I'll say.

I once described my imaginary friend to my wife. She stood patiently while I listed my friend's appearance and attributes.

"William Demarest?" she said.

"Go figure," I said.

"Uncle Charley?"

"Gruff old guy, but a heart of gold," I said.

"That's so sweet, Daddy," my older daughter said.

"Go to your room," her mother ordered.

"Hey guys, Dad's got an imaginary friend," my daughter broadcast to the others. "He's like a grandpa."

My wife, meanwhile, gave me this "I-can't-look-at-you" look. She looked at me, but only through one eye. Like a pirate.

"Let me make sure I have this straight: You have an imaginary friend. He looks like William Demarest?"

I shrugged. "Just my lousy luck, huh?"

"I'm opening the wine," she said, which has become like a mantra for her.

What am I supposed to say? "Yeah, I have a fantasy friend. She's a nubile actress with a perfect little upturned nose." Give me a break. You can't really pick your fantasy friends. In my experience, they pretty much pick you. Besides, you really think William Demarest is going to help me dig a trench?

So by the end of the day, my actual imaginary friend and I are finished with the water main. We carefully replace the sod over the trench. The lawn looks almost untouched, perhaps even better than before. Naturally, my imaginary friend and I are a little grimy from this project. At her suggestion, we hit the shower.

If an imaginary friend isn't your cup of tea, you can cultivate friends in other ways. You can offer them a beer on a hot day. Make jokes about a recent prostate exam. Offer them spare tickets to ball games. Just don't be overt about it. Like in third grade, friendships should mostly just happen.

Good friends call at the right time. They don't mind popping by, and they know just when to leave. They will almost always bring a six-pack.

They will fight for you when threatened, make fun of you when you screw up, prop you up when you're defeated, and give you sensible advice when you don't really want to listen.

Skeptical?

Well, here's my advice to you, my friend: Make as many buddies as possible, both real and imaginary. It's a long life. You'll need every single one.

26

COCK-A-DOODLE . . . DON'T!

THERE IS ALWAYS that magic moment when I return home after a long day, to the open arms and gratitude of the people I toil for all day long.

"Dad, we missed you!" they cry out.

"Daddy, how was your day?"

"Cock!" screams the toddler.

That's his favorite new word: Cock, like the rooster. We think he's trying to say "cat," though he might be trying to say "clock." In either case, when he screams out "cock!" in a crowded restaurant, it seems to generate a lot of sour, disapproving expressions from the people who don't know us. And, of course, laughter from the people who do.

"Cat?" my wife prompts him. "Say caaaaaat, sweetheart."

"Cock!" he screams, then dances a little jig.

It's a high-impact word, cock. We go to great ends to not make a big deal of it, because with a toddler, the second you make a big deal of something is the moment it solidifies in his brain as a trigger word. We've spent many recent meals with our hands over our mouths, trying not to spit out our peas, while the baby sat at the end of the table shouting out the C-word.

"I can't take it," the boy will finally say and go running, hunched, to his bedroom to guffaw out loud.

"Me either," says the older daughter, who will run likewise to her room, doubled over, with iced tea coming out of her pretty nose.

"We've just got to ignore him," his mother says softly and sternly to the rest of us at the table.

"Just don't make a big deal of it," I echo.

"Coooooooooock!" says the baby.

I presume, eventually, that we will all be arrested. We will be in the wrong place at the wrong time, which is how arrests usually happen. We'll be in church on Christmas Eve, or in line at Starbucks, when the toddler shouts out his favorite animal name. People will mistake it for an expletive and haul us off to jail on some sort of trumped up morals charge.

"We think he means 'cat,'" we'll tell the desk sergeant.

"Or maybe 'clock,'" someone else will explain.

"Lock 'em up," the desk sergeant will say, "the whole bunch of them."

Language did not come early to him. He laughed joyfully at an early age, fixed me with his laser eyes and impishly smirked. His first word, at well over a year-old, was ma-ma-ma-ma-ma. For 6 weeks, I tried to get him to say da-da-da, and the best I could get was "ga."

In the meantime, I tried to teach him to brush his teeth. Every time I'd stand at the sink, he'd pull over his little blue stool and stand beside me, digging into the drawer where we keep all the toothbrushes. I'd smear toothpaste on his brush, and the toddler would deftly begin to brush his teeth. It didn't matter that he hadn't had breakfast yet. He wanted to be with Dad.

The only real problem was keeping his mouth closed so the toothpaste wouldn't dribble down his chin and the front of his pajamas. Evidently, closing your lips around a toothbrush to prevent leakage is an acquired skill.

"Careful," I'd say, then wipe his chin with a towel.

"How's it going in there?" my wife would call out from the other room.

"Well, the floor's very minty," I'd explain.

After we brushed our teeth, we'd shave. I'd lather my face first, then bend down to lather his cheeks and chin. Most of the time, he didn't even really need to shave. His skin was soft as custard and about as hairy. But I played along.

"There," I'd say after dabbing his face with shaving cream. "Go show your mom."

And off he'd scamper to show his mother this shaving cream beard. Of all the cutesy, hokey, ridiculous things I do, it's the one I like best.

Then, 20 minutes late for work, I'd make him breakfast. I always find it odd that I, of all people, am teaching the toddler how to eat breakfast, my worst and most hapless meal.

For I'm the sort of guy who's always burning his tongue on the first sip of coffee. It's like I have short-term coffee memory loss, and can't go from one morning to the next without remembering how that first dab against the tongue is unmercifully hot. That's me in a nutshell, punished by my own eagerness to begin the day.

Likewise, I can't begin a donut then not finish it immediately. If, for example, the phone rings after the first bite, I hurriedly shove the rest of the donut in my mouth and begin the phone conversation like a guy trying to swallow a Chihuahua. People have been known to call me just to hear the drowning/donut sounds I produce first thing in the day.

I'd like to be able to put a donut down and walk away. But I can't. Like most men, I'm strong in some ways and weak in others.

This is the man she has chosen to teach her son to eat breakfast.

"What do you want?" I ask him each morning.

"Awful," he says.

Awful is his word for waffle. Ga-ga is his term for egg, which is remarkably close to his word for "dad." I don't know if he thinks of me as an egg or as an egg as a dad, but since it is so close to the subject of roosters, I hesitate to try. I just crack the egg and get on with it.

"Toast?" I ask.

"No," he says and straight arms me like a running back.

Breakfast, by all accounts, is his most difficult meal. He doesn't like blueberries. He doesn't like Jell-O. He'll eat half a Cheerio. I can get only a spoon or two of yogurt down his gullet before he begins to buzz it on his lips and sputter it on my dress shirt.

"No spitting, pal," I warn him.

"No," his mother adds, more sternly.

He is attracted to the oddest things for breakfast. He likes to slurp the juice from what's left of my grapefruit. He likes grape juice all right, but not wine.

"He's got some crazy tastes," I tell his mother.

"Look who's talking," she says.

At 2, however, food is mostly for throwing. The baby prefers things, like little crackers, that are light but aerodynamic. He shares them with the dogs. He shares his pasta with the cat. The animals wait around his high chair like those kids who wait outside Wrigley Field for home runs to land in the street. The pets then scurry ruthlessly for whatever he has thrown, a riot of frantic paws.

"Out!" I yell to the animals, who will slink behind the couch for a minute or two, then slowly work their way back toward his chair.

"Out!" I scream, when I see their snouts reappear around the legs of the table.

We feed the baby well and often, with perhaps 5 percent of all food actually making it into his mouth. Of this 5 percent, only a tiny bit makes it all the way to his stomach. Most times, he sucks the flavor from whatever tiny morsel he is chewing before spitting it out on his dish. He is the only child we've had who eats one molecule at a time.

"I don't know what to do," his mother worries constantly. "He's so skinny."

My prediction is that he will not let himself starve. That he still smashes enough fistfuls of mashed potatoes into his mouth and cheeks to sustain himself, even if not all of it makes it into his tummy, which must be the size of a beer cap.

My prediction is that he will grow tall and strong—almost all of our other children are either taller than my wife and me or appear headed that way.

My prediction is that by the time he is 12, he will be able to hit a baseball farther than me, do more somersaults off the high dive, consume more $8 hot dogs at a single Dodger game.

I'm not too worried about the little guy's eating habits. Before we know it, he'll be 6-foot-2 and carrying the Christmas tree into the house on his shoulder. Let's hope, anyway.

"Bye-bye, little guy," I say as I prepare to go off to work.

He smiles, wraps a sticky hand around my neck. Squeezes with all his might. The cat pounces on a piece of waffle she finds on the floor.

"Cock!" says the little boy, profoundly delighted.

Being Irish, I have been exposed to a lot of bad language in my life. Sometimes, it seems the Irish have only two emotions, agony and ecstasy. In either case, they curse joyfully and with abandon, a reflex much like breathing.

My own father, a mild-mannered man except in a car, would curse before putting the key in the ignition each morning, knowing fully well that he would soon be stuck in traffic. The advance knowledge of this would turn the back of his neck red and make his fingers tremble. Elsewhere, he was like John Kennedy—charming and cool. In a car, he was a linebacker, scouring the world for running backs.

My father may have, in fact, invented road rage, though I never saw him actually assault anyone, and I doubt he ever did. He was in his prime just when America discovered freeways weren't so much a solution as a curse. By then, he'd heavily invested in the suburbs and felt trapped. So it wasn't the jerk who just cut him off that he was so angry at. It was his own foolishness, for abandoning the city he loved for smog-choked farm roads.

It was in his car—a '67 Chevy Impala—that I learned to curse. Sure, my 10-year-old friends knew and shared some big juicy cuss words, but nobody could string them together like my old man. He would spew them with such machine-gun-like precision that all you could do was admire it and smile, while our mother winced and looked out her own window.

In college, my cursing improved, and then as a sportswriter, I pretty much mastered the art. By the time I was 22, I had a vocabulary of perhaps a thousand words, 800 of which were profane.

As a father myself, I tried to put a lid on such expressiveness. For the Irish, giving up cursing is a little like giving up booze. Swearing is what we do to keep the tops of our heads from blowing off. If there were AA meetings for curse-o-holics, I would've happily attended.

Little by little, I improved, so that by the time we had teenagers, bad language was pretty much prohibited in our house. Sometimes, I'd hear them on the phone, through their bedroom doors, as they used the salty language of young adolescence. I ignored it as long as it didn't make it out of their bedroom.

Now, after decades of censorship and self-discipline, I have a toddler who, quite innocently, uses one of the most unacceptable words in our society.

I stifle laughter, but I can't stifle smiles. How amusing is a life that comes so full circle? My dad passed away more than 10 years ago, yet I listen to the toddler calling the cat and can't help but hear him.

Dad, if that's you in there somewhere, just stop it, okay? You're gonna get us all arrested.

27

A USER'S GUIDE TO EARTH

WELCOME TO our planet. We hope you have a pleasant stay here and find Earth to be someplace you'd return to regularly or recommend to friends. You won't find it listed in the Zagat's guide. But we've worked very hard to make Earth comfortable. You should've seen it before we invented concrete. It was a dump, basically.

Back then, you could travel 100 miles without running into a Denny's. There was no trash pickup. When someone was done with dinner, they just threw it into the bushes, where some hungry pterodactyl would find it later.

There was no takeout food. No dry cleaners. No guns. No police. You can imagine how dangerous it was. Our planet's about 4.5 billion years old, but as recently as 3,000 to 4,000 years ago, you still couldn't find a decent burger. Pizza had yet to be invented. *60 Minutes* wasn't even on. Sunday night, people just sat around and talked to one another.

Then came the Greeks, who invented sarcasm, and the Romans, who invented greed. Did you know that at one time, the Romans lost the formula for cement? Idiots. And they were considered smart, at least as Earthlings go.

Now everybody has cement, even the most backward of nations. Most anyone can buy a gun, or a shoulder-fired missile launcher. Yet, we are safer now than ever, with vast armies of law enforcement personnel to tend the public safety. When that doesn't work, we have vast armies of armies to do the job. When there are no wars, we often make them up.

We are the most advanced civilization of all time. Did you know there are 200 varieties of ice cream alone? You can get breakfast at almost any hour, at least in our major cities. Sick? You won't be for long.

We have more doctors, more diagnostic equipment, more medicine than at any time in human history. Last year, 5 million children starved to death.

If you happen to have it, we still need a cure for cancer, AIDS, and the common cold. You could make a fortune just wiping out herpes. But we've got plastic surgery whipped. If you're unhappy at all with your breasts or your buttocks, just raise your green and scaly hand.

While here, be careful around rivers and oceans. They can be surprisingly swift and deep. There are some lifeguards on duty, but they usually leave by 5, right about the time you've poured your first cocktail.

Likewise, use caution around power lines. Stay clear of nuclear towers and fraternity houses.

Don't waste your time with TV—you could spend a lifetime searching for a decent show—and attend movies sparingly. If you want a few hours of mild entertainment, check out the local college's production of *Hamlet* or *The Music Man*. You'll find more laughs.

Just a warning that you'll find some of our electronics difficult to use and cell phones are buzzing just everywhere. Feel free to crush them with the heel of your space boots. Trust me, no one will complain.

Never, ever, ever, ever, ever buy something on the first day you go out looking, whether it be a car or a house. Shop around. When redoing the kitchen, get at least three bids. At least.

And never, ever, ever, ever, ever, ever, ever marry the first woman you kiss. Unless you really like her. Our women are attractive, though occasionally spoiled. Don't expect to get out of a restaurant with one for under 100 bucks, not including wine. Most are sexually voracious and prefer to mate for life, even though their prime only lasts 60 or 70 years. So beware of women and the men who dress like them. Don't say I didn't warn you.

If you decide to have kids here, be sure to wait till you're 30, after you're secure in your job and have established decent credit. Any younger, and you'll be forced to grow up while they do, which is a tricky maneuver, to say the least. Best you grow up first, and then have kids.

Another note on the children here: They appear docile at first, but are in fact our most dangerous wildlife. Never take a long car trip with one, or debate the merits of weekly chores. Life's too short.

While here, be sure to check out many of our local attractions. The

Atlantic Ocean, for one. The Poles are nice, though a little chilly in summer. Be sure to see Disney World. Paris and Florence have several fine museums.

To get anywhere, you'll probably have to go through Dallas or Dubai. Our airports aren't our proudest achievements. We put more thought into the average American shopping mall.

Steer clear of the Middle East, eastern Europe, and any American expressway. Rush hour now lasts from 6 in the morning to about 9 at night. After that, you'll hit a little stop and go. Be especially wary of uninsured drivers, which is virtually everyone in L.A., and starlets talking on their cell phones. There are many tourists—like you, new to the city—who have entered LA's downtown interchanges and never emerged.

Seats of government are interesting for a while, but the British Parliament tends to be long-winded, and the politics of America is largely done behind closed doors, no matter what everyone says.

Note that our most capable people aren't in the halls of government or in some fancy boardroom. If you want wisdom, talk to a guy on a tractor. He'll chat reluctantly. A good quality in a man.

Food? You can get a good burger in Chicago, great Italian food in St. Louis, and in Miami, the most succulent stone crab you've ever tasted. If you want a kind word, though, try one of our smaller towns—places like Hannibal, Missouri, or Pekin, Illinois.

The big news of the last 100 years? World War II is over, polio is cured, Elvis is dead. Who's Elvis? Only the biggest single name of the last century. You should've seen him sing. You should've seen him eat.

In other major news, diapers are now disposable, they've cloned a sheep, music is free (and you get what you pay for).

In fact, if you can do anything about the current state of our popular music, your efforts would elevate you to cult status (see Elvis note above), and we'd probably grant you the deed to any major city of your choosing. Don't automatically pick New York or London. Milwaukee is nice, especially in autumn. Honestly, take your pick though. We'd trade all our cities for one decent, humable tune.

Till then, we hope you have an excellent stay here on our little planet. Please make yourself at home. There are extra towels in the closet.

Check out time is noon.

28

THE MAN WHO CAN'T SAY NO

BY NOW you're probably wondering: "Why isn't this book better? I thought this guy was supposed to find the magic in everyday things. I'm just not seeing the magic."

Here's why.

Too often, as I sat in the bedroom writing this, they never left me alone. Never. In fact, as I write these words now, they are huddled around me, blowing up pool toys for a joyous afternoon in the neighbor's back-yard. I think one is chewing on my toe. No wait, that's the dog.

In blowing up the pool toys, the kids quickly deplete the oxygen in the room, and they are soon all a little high, wearing the pool toys on their heads and somersaulting around the bed. The toddler climbs my lap and grabs a handful of my T-shirt, and in the process, a fair amount of chest hair. I may have mentioned that my chest hair is rampant and surprisingly tender. When he twists my T-shirt, doves cry.

You think James Joyce could keep a train of thought under these conditions? I can't hardly spell train under these . . . wait, where was I? Oh, that's right. I was apologizing about the book. Sigh.

Every time I get a little something going, the dog brings something mysterious into the house, or the baby needs a fresh diaper. I plead for privacy, but then there's another diaper. When I am done changing him, the toddler always shakes my hand and says "thank you." A sucker for good manners, I usually play along.

Another reason this book is not better may sound familiar to you. You know how you sometimes volunteer for things you don't really want to do? I'm not just talking about helping to sandbag the town when the river approaches flood stage. Or even marriage. I'm talking about school fund-raisers and town beautification projects. The sort of thing that involves 3-hour committee meetings at the library or coffee at someone's house when all you want is your *Sports Illustrated* and a beer. Nobody really wants to do these things. We do them for the same reason we do many things: guilt. Never underestimate the power of guilt. Guilt gets us out of bed in the morning. And to the office by 9.

Flattery is a powerful stimulant as well. What these committee chairpersons usually do is seduce you with a flattering remark, which makes you want to believe everything that person says to you. Then the chairperson explains how much they really need you to take some volunteer position, because you're the most-qualified, wonderful person they've ever run across. Believe me, the chairperson insists, we're both a little above such tasks. But if we don't do these things, who will?

That's when the guilt begins to kick in. How can you let down a person who thinks so highly of you? In a suburb, people fall sucker to such tactics all the time. Which is how I came to coach the little girl's all-star team.

"Huh?" I say into the phone.

"This is Terry," the voice on the phone says.

"Oh hi," I say.

"Is this the famous writer?" Terry says.

I get this a lot. I am famous to about 20 people, all of whom seem to need something from me.

"No," I say into the phone.

"Funny piece this morning," Terry says.

Terry is a genius at these things. Once, in trying to persuade me to speak at a coaching clinic, he compared me to the great sportswriter Jim Murray. But he didn't stop there. He said I played checkers like Gandhi and ate oysters like Orson Welles. You don't get to be league commissioner for nothing. Terry knows how to pour it on.

"So, the softball board met last night," he says.

"That must've been exciting," I say.

"They want you to coach the all-star team," Terry says.

Now, understand that there are men and women in our twisted little town who would sell their spouses in exchange for coaching the all-star team. They fall to sleep at night dreaming of whipping Sierra Madre or El Rio, the teams that dominate all-star softball in Southern California. I, meanwhile, go to sleep dreaming of banana cream pie.

Which brings us to Rule No. 1 in the Book of Life: The less you crave something, the more likely you are to get it. And if you really, really want something, such desperation seems to make it harder to attain. It is for that reason, I get so little pie.

"So will you do it?" Terry asks.

"I've got a lot of stuff going," I explain.

Here is Rule No. 2 in the Book of Life: The more coy you are, the more they want you.

"It's just a few tournaments," Terry explains.

Sure, a few tournaments. One will be in Death Valley. Another will be in a weeded lot adjacent to Folsom State Prison. The third will be on a sun-baked portion of Venus. All nice places to play softball in July.

"So you'll do it?" Terry says. "Lydia is very excited."

Lydia is Terry's daughter, a promising left-handed hitter who never looks all that excited to me. But she can whack the heck out of a softball. She can play catcher, too, if you need her to.

"Who's pitching?" I ask.

"Caitlin can pitch," Terry says.

Notice the wording. Caitlin can pitch but will she? What's her daddy demanding in return? A spot on the coaching staff? A new Lexus?

"You'll have to call him," Terry says.

So I spend a week trying to call Mark, who is a busy dentist with three kids and a thousand things to do. Finally, he calls me back. Caitlin's playing somewhere else, he says.

Which is bad news of course. Without Caitlin, we're left with little Alex, a brave and promising right-hander with a killer curveball. But she can't carry the team alone. You need a second pitcher. You need Caitlin.

"Caitlin's playing somewhere else," I tell the board and return to writing my book. This book. The one that should be better.

Thing is, I love coaching. I started when the boy was small. You should've seen his T-ball league. No kidding, one kid in his league just signed with the Angels for a million bucks. These little dudes could play.

One year, we were the Cubs. The next year, we were also the Cubs. We overcame this bad karma to field some very competitive teams.

Like anyone new to something they don't understand, I took my coaching responsibilities quite seriously. I carefully put together practice plans to make sure we covered the fundamentals. Before each game, I'd study a lineup card with the care and passion of someone doctoring a good Bloody Mary.

"I have an offer for you," a league official offered after a successful season ended.

"No," I said, wise even then to the tender traps of coaching.

"There's a girls' team that wants to play you," he said.

Maybe it was because we were the Cubs, and they thought we would be an easy target. Maybe it was the spirited way my son and his buddies played the game of competitive T-ball. Whatever it was, this team of girls wanted to play us bad.

"Of course," I told the official. "Bring 'em on."

This Battle of the Sexes was to take place at our league's end-of-season picnic. This is the festive carnival-like day in the park, where kids compete in sack races, relay races and—in a little ceremony toward the end—receive their trophies. Men who have no business around a microphone take the stage to introduce their teams and hand out the gleaming plastic trophies. It is a splendid day. Lasts about 19 hours.

The final event that day was our exhibition game against the girls. My team, made up of 5- and 6-year-olds, spent warmups drinking root-beer floats and making ice cream sundaes in their navels. I thought for a moment our best player, a Latino kid named Ciro, gashed his arm. Turned out to be melted Popsicle running from his shoulder to his elbow.

"I'll be all right, Coach," he told me.

"Anyone seen my beer?" asked the shortstop.

Meanwhile, our opponents—a dozen little girls in ponytails and tucked-in shirts—spent the warmups doing perfect jumping jacks at the far side of the field.

"Uh-oh," I told my assistant coach.

"What?"

"Look at that," I said, pointing to our opponents.

"Whoaaaaa," he moaned, looking up from the biggest root-beer float I've ever seen.

Of course, there were 300 spectators at our game, all there to cheer for the underdog girls, who in fact should've been seen as clear favorites. They cheered the girls, and some of the dads—true louts—actually booed the boys. Our friendly little exhibition had turned into some sort of epic battle between good and evil. We'd been ambushed. Never, before or since, have I ever wanted to win a game so much.

The boys, bless their candied hearts, were brave and strong. We took an early lead, and I finally was able to breathe again. The girls were good and more intense than we were, but never underestimate the importance of three hot dogs in your belly. At the end of two innings, we were up, 4–0.

Then digestion set in, a process in the American male that can be quite debilitating. First, the stomach turns upside down to empty itself. Then the colon goes to work like a giant anaconda swallowing a toaster. The rest of the body shuts down during this process. Including, apparently, the brain and the eyelids.

I looked over at our dugout at one point, and it looked like a trauma unit. One kid's belly was heaving as if he were giving birth. Three kids had passed out from sugar shock. One was hurling. The outfielders were in a little circle, having their stomachs pumped.

The girls' team, meanwhile, was dancing around the bases as if celebrating a wedding. Evidently, they hadn't consumed four hot dogs apiece at lunch and washed it down with 20 ounces of whipped cream. As the crowd roared, they took a 1-run lead.

"We're toast," I told my assistant coach.

"Did someone say toast?" asked our first baseman.

In our last ups, with 300 spectators cheering the girls' every move, our first baseman Ciro—since dubbed "Ciro the Hero"—smashed a line drive that drove in the winning run, giving us the win and preserving the boys' self-esteem—though I suspect such things to be overrated. Had they been beaten by the girls, the boys may well have been better served in the long run. The lesson: Don't take any opponent lightly, no matter how many feet of Red Bullet licorice you've wolfed down before the game.

As my son grew older, I continued to coach him. When he was 8, I bought him a glove as big as a T-bone steak. For 2 years, he used it as a pillow. As close as possible to his dreams.

The boy and I played catch over and over in the driveway. A million fast balls. A thousand curveballs in the dirt.

"Watch this, Dad," he'd say.

"Okay, I'm ready," I'd say.

He'd start to grip the ball as if examining a snow globe. He'd look at it close to find the right seams. He'd get his fingers just so.

"Clunnnnnnnk."

"Oops," the boy would say.

There's a mailbox at the end of the driveway. Usually, I could just reach in and push the dent out.

"Wanna see my slider?" the boy would say.

"Sure," I'd say.

"Clunnnnnk," said the mailbox.

To this day, the boy and I still play catch in the driveway. He is 19 now and has muscles like ship rope. I have to caution him to take it a little easy on the throws. He still hits the mailbox. It still goes clunk. But now, the dents go far deeper. Pretty soon I'm going to have to call a body shop.

"Wanna see my changeup?" he asks.

"Of course," I say.

A changeup is a wonderful pitch. It is thrown with the same fury as a fastball. But the pitcher palms the ball, which makes it travel far slower. The batter, spotting the same arm whip as a fastball, reacts quickly, often swinging a second before the ball floats across the plate. I like changeups. A good changeup makes a batter look like a drunk swinging comically at a cop. Best of all, a changeup doesn't take my head off.

"Clunnnnnnnk."

"Nice pitch," I tell the boy.

"Thanks," he says.

So now I coach the little girl. Softball is different from baseball, but not as different as little boys and little girls. The girls listen better. But they won't lay out for grounders the way the boys will.

"Get your uniforms dirty!" I yell, when a ball skips past them in the infield. "Go hard or go home."

Remember that all-star thing I mentioned earlier? It worked out after all, of course. I thought I was off the hook, but we were able to drum up some pitching from a neighboring league—a merger I was sure was illegal but turned out not so. Building an all-star team is a little like testing anti-trust legislation. When you think you've spotted the most illegal, egregious activity, it turns out to be perfectly okay.

Our team of little mercenaries finished second and third in the two tournaments we entered. Instead of working on this book, I was spending every afternoon and weekend on the dustiest, hottest softball fields you've ever seen.

Now, somehow, we're in the state finals. I have been coaching, continuously, for 12 straight years, with barely a break between softball, baseball, and soccer. It could all end right now, and I'd be content—happy to go home and bask in the air-conditioning, to work on this book that means so much to me.

But we keep winning here at state. Rule No. 3 in the Book of Life: When you've had enough of a kid's sports season, they extend it by winning playoff games.

With each win, we push further into the playoff bracket. Friday becomes Saturday. Saturday becomes Sunday. The girls have turned our hotel into a giant slumber party. The desk clerks literally quiver when we return at the end of each day. The final straw was when the girls realized they could charge snacks, soft drinks, and coffee to their rooms.

Me? I have been out in the sun now for 3 straight days. You could bake brownies in my boxers. You could roast popcorn in my ears. I'm not sure what sport we're playing. But I know we're behind. And I have a book deadline approaching. Wait, Abby just singled. Hey, maybe we're not done yet.

I coach because I can't say no. I coach because I love it, and it helps me squeeze the most from this second childhood. Or is it my third childhood? Wait, maybe it's my fourth.

Back home, meanwhile, there's a 2-year-old boy. Throws right. Bats right. He thinks dragonflies are helicopters and lightning bugs are angels.

I think he shows a lot of promise.

29

THE LITTLE FACE IN THE BATTING HELMET

TODAY, I COACHED you for the last time, on a dusty little field near San Diego, where you let a fly ball drop in front of you as if watching a grasshopper land. We lost the playoff game, but I don't really care. Because it was the last time I will ever coach you, and that's the memorable thing right now. Next year, you'll go on to play for your school team. For the first time in your athletic career, you'll be coached by strangers, while I watch enviously from the stands.

It's been a good run, though. Several championships. Lots of playoff runs and close calls, in soccer and in softball. Remember that shootout kick you missed in the semifinals 2 years ago? Not me. I'm so over that. I'm so over that you wouldn't believe it.

I will remember you, always, as the little face in the batting helmet. You are growing tall and beautiful and graceful and sophisticated, yet it is that little girl's face in the batting helmet that I will remember most. And the way you used to boss me around back then when you were 4, like a tiny Katharine Hepburn. You were always wise beyond your years, and dare I say now, too often right.

I will remember the way that—hardly out of diapers—you joined your first baseball team, which featured the thing you dreaded most: little boys. You batted seventh on the team, ahead of six of your male teammates.

I will remember how at the very first practice, one of the other coaches asked each of you to say your names, at which point you burst into tears. It was so unlike you that for a moment, your mother and I didn't really know what to do. Should we comfort you or just let you stand there and wipe your embarrassment away with your sleeve till you realized how silly you were acting? We chose to comfort you, and at the next practice you were fine.

I will remember your first day of kindergarten. You were dressed in a shiny backpack and brand new shoes, your hair in pigtails. You couldn't wait to go to kindergarten, you couldn't wait to get on with your life.

I remember the Thanksgiving play when you were one of the only kids who knew all the words to the songs. That day, the grandparents were invited, and I remember them marveling at the little red-haired girl in the front row, the one who sang out every word.

I will remember the writing competition you won in fourth grade and the way you walked proudly to the front of the cafeteria to read your winning work. All I could think was, "Crap, another writer," but you stood there proudly before a big room full of parents and without a stutter, read your piece as calmly as if you were ordering lunch. "She'll never be a writer," I thought then, a little relieved.

I remember teaching you to tell time, to tie your shoes, to cast a fishing line. I remember the way you first gripped a softball, palming it like you were about to open an orange. "Gentler," I urged. "And with the fingertips."

I will remember how you used to hold the tongs when I barbecued or spilled the latex when I painted the porch. The way you scooped out pumpkins. The way you reached all the way in, up to your bony shoulder, till you had pumpkin clear to your ears.

I will remember the way the August sun brought out your freckles, and connected them together. I remember how pale you were the day you were born.

I will remember how you always had more friends around on Friday nights than anyone I have ever known. The way you ran for the phone. The first time a boy called. "Yuck Finn," I called him. "Oh, Daaaaaad!" you said.

I will remember explaining why we lied to you about Santa Claus for so many years. A rational kid, prone to questions, you valued truth and consistency from your parents, when all we wanted to give you was a little magic to light your earliest days. Silly us.

I will remember how in the fifth grade, you announced you wanted to be a doctor, specializing in orthopedics.

"Good, because this knee has been giving me trouble," I told you.

"Which knee?" you asked.

Which knee? Well, it's the one you used to bounce on as a baby. The one I kneeled on while teaching you to catch. The one you kicked with your hard dress shoes while I held you in church. The one you grabbed at in that haunted house I built for you when you were 3.

Now, you stand before a hallway mirror, getting ready for some activity with your friends. To a dad, a teenaged daughter is like a car wreck. We try not to watch, yet we cannot look away. You may not realize it, but we watch you out of the corner of our sports sections.

Your right bangs, you brush 50 times; the left bangs, 50 more. You keep pulling at your waistline, at some layer of clothing beneath that I do not fully understand.

The little Irish face is sharper now. There is mascara. I used to put eye black on your cheeks to ward off the sun before softball games, the only makeup I know. Your mother taught you all the other stuff. Why, I'll never know.

In the mirror, there's a girl, almost 14 now and taller and prettier with every new day. You glide through the door now and I can't tell whether it's you or your college-aged sister. Oops, you're taller than your big sister. When did that happen? Quit feeding her, okay?

You stand in the mirror, pretty as a Haydn concerto, softer than an April rain. I am prouder now than the day you were born.

But to me, you will always be that little face in the batting helmet—giggling at your daddy, swinging for the moon.

It was then I loved the best.

FAVORITE COLUMNS
FROM THE PAST

A COLUMN is a gift, and I am grateful each week to write one for the *Los Angeles Times*, where columns are not exactly handed out like lollipops. What follows are 12 or so greatest hits, based on the reaction they received and my own sense of what makes a newspaper column memorable. They were selected from the more than 400 weekly pieces that have appeared in the *Los Angeles Times* and other newspapers around the world since the column began in 1998. I'd like to thank the *Times* for allowing me to include them here.

AH . . . AUTUMN

IT IS A FALL DAY. A perfect day. Some complain that the after-noon air is too cool, but we've been sun-blasted hot here in the foothills for five long months. The cool feels good. Like brushing your teeth. Like a snowy kiss.

We need this hint of winter. It herds us toward each other in substantial ways. Toward a kitchen, where soup is simmering.

Yes, I'm making soup. I would make soup even if I didn't like soup. I turn on a football game, I chop some garlic, I boil some water and add a ham bone and some beans. Soup. It's that easy.

The people I live with, the ones I care about most, are not around. It is pleasantly quiet in ways it seldom ever is. You can hear the floorboards creak. The snap of a brass lockset in a good heavy door. House sounds. In the corner, a dog snores softly.

I pour a soft drink over shaved ice. I turn down the sound on the game and put on a Todd Rundgren album. It reminds me of college and the papers I didn't finish. Turns out that finishing stuff is overrated.

> "I'll come around to see you once in a while,
> Or if I ever need a reason to smile . . ."

On TV, the Giants and Cowboys are going into overtime. Somebody loses a helmet. A place kicker practices into a net. I have seen this a thousand times, the closing seconds of a tight ballgame. In heaven, all games go to overtime.

During a Dallas drive, I sample the soup. Needs salt. I add salt. Needs oregano. I add oregano. I had a bad experience with oregano once. It was worse than being mugged. I sprinkle it carefully. Cooking with oregano is like cooking with gunpowder.

In the bedroom, a teenager stirs. He hasn't been sleeping; he's been hibernating. He is a *Zits* cartoon. He is a James Dean movie. I offer him soup. He scratches his head and mumbles, "I-dunno-I-think-I'd rather-have-cereal." Kids.

I make a fire. It is the first fire of fall, the best fire of fall. I throw in a couple of pinecones to juice the air, and an issue of the *New Yorker* that I didn't much care for. Overrated, the *New Yorker*. Too long. Too repetitive. Like a friend of a friend who won't leave.

The people I live with return. They have been out buying a home-coming dress for the little girl. It's a mystery why a little girl needs a homecoming dress since she's still a little girl and will always be my little girl. I refuse to let her grow up. Kids are the opposite of wine. They don't always improve with age. In the meantime, the toddler sits in the living room, content to play with the dust particles floating in a shard of October sunlight.

"You should see my dress, Daddy," the little girl says.

It's a green dress, the color of martini olives. Macy's, probably. Or maybe the National Guard.

"I don't know if I like this dress," she says, trying it on again.

In my experience, there are two times a woman tries on a dress, in the store and again at home. One has nothing to do with the other. The fact that she liked it in the store will have absolutely no bearing on whether she likes it in her bedroom.

"That dress looks adorable," her mother insists.

"I hate my hair," the little girl says, though it is the color of chestnuts and hangs like expensive linen.

There is the threat of tears. The little girl hates her hair so much, they go out looking for another dress.

"I love her hair," I tell the soup.

"We can't play this game anymore..." says Todd Rundgren.

There'll be soup here when they get home. And a fire. And a football game. Bread, warm from the oven, sprinkled with Parmesan cheese.

The kids will come into the house, since it's too cool and drizzly to stay outside, or to go to the beach, or to hang at some friend's Jacuzzi—all the usual activities that lure children away from the house in warmer months, which are glorious but disruptive. Fun but fractured.

Today, instead, they'll come inside because the house smells of pumpkins and soup, like a country diner on a frosty day. Like a family cabin in the woods.

That's why we like fall.

The happiest pirate on Earth

LIKE A LOT OF DADS, I have a love-hate relationship with Disneyland. First, I can never get past a bad stock purchase I made back when Disney hired Ovitz and I thought it would rule the world.

"We have that on our 'buy' list," my broker said at the time.

"Then let's be bold about it," I told her.

Savvy move. I no longer invest in Disney stock. Instead, we just come down to the Magic Kingdom and throw big wads of cash in the air. It's cheaper that way.

I also have had some interesting experiences at Disneyland. A mother—there's no better term—once pushed a baby stroller up my Achilles tendon and almost to my buttocks, at which point she realized that she had pushed a stroller on to the buttocks of a man she didn't know and backed off a little, out of sheer courtesy.

"That feels so good," I said at the time, or words to that effect.

That's the hate part.

Mostly, I love Disneyland, the colors, the crowds, even the lines. Nope, I don't even mind standing in line with sweaty strangers hour after hour, the blood pooling in my ankles. It's a small price to pay for precious time with the kids.

"What's your name again?" I ask one of them.

"Who?"

"You."

"Mom!"

Oops, wrong kid. Oh, our kids are over there, running wild on Main Street U.S.A. They are walk-skipping with a woman who has two cameras bouncing on her hip. Cecil B. DeMom: my wife, my costar, my cinematographer.

"Come on, Dad!" someone says.

"Hurry," says Cecil B. DeMom.

As you may have heard, Disneyland is now 50, but doesn't look it. Not a day over 45, in fact. Disneyland is sort of like Michelle Pfeiffer. You know she's getting up there but don't really want to know how far.

"Think they'll let me fish here?" I ask the little girl while we wait for a boat at It's a Small World.

"Dad!"

"I'm just asking," I explain.

Small World has a holiday theme going, which dampens the head-banging repetition of the usual "Small World" lyrics, a song that has prompted many men to leap to their deaths. Not today. Today, we see what Christmas is like in Africa and, I think, Norway. Though it might've been upper Minnesota. You know, the iron range region up around Duluth.

"Where next?" asks my lovely and patient older daughter.

"Thunder Mountain?" I suggest, and they pat me on the back like I just won at bingo.

What I've always appreciated about Disneyland is that it is one of the few public venues without a scent. There is almost no smell. Just a wondrous blandness that captures the essence of the place.

"Hey, look at the lake," I say as we near Frontierland.

"That's a river," corrects a worker with a broom and a dustpan.

"Whatever," I say.

"See them ducks?" he says, pointing to a dozen mallards.

"You do much hunting here?" I ask.

"Honey?" he asks.

"No, hunting," I say.

"Honey?" he says, brow bending, wondering if he should make some sort of arrest.

"Dad, let's go," says one of the kids, who are always interfering when I'm trying to make new friends.

Now, a lot of amazing things have happened to me: marriage, children, steady employment. But nothing tops what happened to us next. We walked right up and boarded Pirates of the Caribbean. Wait time? Zilch.

"I don't believe this," my wife says.

"Take a picture!" says the little girl.

Pirates is a sensational ride, of course, featuring thievery, debauchery, fires, and cannon fights. Naturally, I find the romance in the moment.

"Stop it!" scolds Cecil B. DeMom when I get a little grabby.

"Stop what?" I ask.

"I'll scream," she warns.

"Arrrgh!" I say, though I noticed on the next turn, she leaned into me a little. Women. They're always attracted to the bad pirate.

"Arrrgh," says the toddler.

"Don't push your luck," I tell him.

The rest of the evening is pretty much a blur. We watched a parade where all I could think about was how cold that poor mermaid must've been.

"She's got a leotard," explained someone nearby. Whew.

Then we waited for the tram to the parking garage for at least 45 minutes, a little uncertain about where we parked.

Three days later we were still there, wandering the parking lot, looking for the white minivan. Any white minivan. Just something to hot-wire and get out of there.

We spent Christmas Day in that huge parking garage, wandering like Wise Men, swearing we'd never make a rookie mistake like that again. Because by then, most everyone else had found their cars, returned home, and were opening gifts.

"Thanks, Dad," the little girl said when we finally left.

Arrrgh. Love Disneyland. Love it.

A LITTLE CHURCH, A LITTLE CHILI

THE FULL MOON is coming up up over the mountains like a big bowl of milk, and friends and neighbors are all entering church for Christmas Eve services. As the baby sits on my lap, I try to re-crease his cotton collar with my thumb and forefinger. Lots of luck.

"You look good in church," I tell him.

"Who doesn't?" he answers.

Of course, everybody looks good in church. The soft light. The stained glass. If I owned a nightclub, I'd copy this flattering look, invite the masses, and collect my fortune.

"Please reach into your pocket..." the pastor says.

"Already?" I think to myself.

"And pull out your keys..." he says.

"Great, now they want my car," I tell my wife.

"Nobody would want your car," she whispers.

"And shake your keys as we all sing 'Jingle Bells,'" the pastor urges.

Hundreds strong, we rise to sing "Jingle Bells." Admittedly, I never really believed in the concept of a one-horse open sleigh. To pull a sleigh properly, you need at least two horses, young and strong. But I play along. It's Christmas.

> Bells on Bob-Tail ring,
> making spirits bright,
> What fun it is to ride and sing
> a sleighing song tonight...

I carry the congregation in song for a while, till I get short of breath, then just lip-sync. In my arms, the baby is jingling his older sister's car keys. A little cylinder of Mace, attached to the key chain, dangles in front of my eyes.

It occurs to me that this could easily turn out to be a very memorable Christmas Eve: the one when I got Maced in church.

We are a Catholic-Lutheran-Presbyterian-Irish-Italian-Ukrainian clan, with a splash of German blood thrown on top, like vermouth.

Belonging to this many factions—at one time or another—is a little like having too many credit cards in your wallet. For now, though, we have settled on this beautiful Presbyterian church. On Christmas Eve, they offer five services.

"Which service?" my wife asked earlier in the day.

"The Packers won't be done till 3," I warned.

"We'll go at 4," she said with a sigh.

Tone-deaf but loud, I now sit on the end of the row so as not to poison the beautiful carols. I seem to be surrounded by well-dressed men who always seem to have $100 bills in their pockets.

How liberating that must be to always have an extra hundred handy for a good haircut or a round of golf. I make a mental note to work harder next year.

"This is such a nice church," says a visitor.

"We really like it," I say.

The Christmas Eve service moves swiftly. It is mostly music, mostly performed by kids. It is a party atmosphere, free of guilt, blame, shame, abashment, and other wicked tools some faiths seem to rely upon.

Gentle as lambs, we end one portion of the service by singing happy birthday, dear Jesus. Happy birthday to you.

Like you, I could do without all the holiday hype. The overspending. The traffic. But Lord I love Christmas Eve. The best buzz in town.

Speaking of alcohol, I remember my father putting together toys for my younger sisters, the tremble in his fingers that urbane men get when they try to do something with their hands.

He could pour a martini without a flinch, but you'd dread the moment he picked up a screwdriver. Big Irish face, like Charles Durning, down on the carpet grunting and cursing the poor saps who wrote the directions.

As a kid, I remember friends coming by. The phone ringing. Dogs jumping at the door. To this day, I believe a good Christmas Eve is part magic, part turmoil.

So at home later, my wife and I have a few coworkers over to tip a glass and enjoy chili and turmoil.

Oh, and of course Christmas tamales. With a spoon of chili over them, tamales are among our finer local delicacies, and one of the best meals you can find. Outside of a ballpark, anyway.

"I wonder if they eat chili in Chile," someone wonders, giving you a sample of the level of our party rhetoric.

"Anybody seen *Spanglish*?" I ask. "Anybody?"

"I'm still looking for one person who's seen *Joey*," my buddy Tom says. "Just one person."

As is usually the case, Christmas Eve goes by too quickly. Good songs. Spicy food. Fast company. At one point, the baby drops his trousers and parades around the living room clucking like a duck and hugging people he barely knows. His eyes collect the candlelight. Everybody laughs.

"How much did he drink?" I ask my wife.

"Have you seen the cat?" she asks.

Cluck-cluck, the baby says, then smooches my buddy Vic hard on the lips. Last spotted, the baby was shimmying up the Christmas tree, hunting for grouse.

Each December, we hurl ourselves at Christmas, wagering that God has a sense of humor...a wry eye...a tolerance for human foible.

Lord help us if we're wrong.

She's really 21?

HERE WE ARE at some overprice Pasadena saloon, celebrating the older daughter's 21st birthday. That's right, 21. Blackjack.

"My first drink," she says giddily to her mother.

Yeah, right. Your first drink? As my buddy Irv says: Why don't you pull my other leg for a while?

"Grandma, what's in a martini?" the older daughter asks.

She's seeking martini advice from my mother-in-law, in from Florida for this birthday milestone. It's like asking Mozart about concertos. Jim Murray about metaphors.

"Gin and vermouth," Grandma explains.

"Yum," the older daughter says.

"Yum," says her little sister.

I study the big menu. It looks like a tax form. I'm no fan of restaurant menus with too many choices. Ideally, there should be one obvious choice, and the other choices should be things like kitty litter, walnut shells, and yesterday's gum. That way I can order that one good thing with the knowledge that I have made the right decision.

Because inevitably in a restaurant, I order something, then have diner's remorse. If I order pasta, I suddenly crave steak. If I order shrimp, I immediately want lamb.

"Grandma, what's vermouth?" the older daughter asks.

My older daughter is sitting at the other end of the table, with a drink that is the color of atomically active dish soap. It is some exotic island drink that no doubt tastes like a piece of coconut pie. There is an umbrella in it. I guess in case it rains.

She hails from a family of accomplished drinkers. Irish clear up to our eyeballs, we take to alcohol the way some families take to golf or politics. When we cry, there is whiskey in our tears.

Indeed, tomorrow I will explain to her all the misery that too much of a good thing can bring to a life. The fractured relationships. The physical and emotional toll. Then again, by tomorrow this little rum drink she is swilling may explain it all.

"And, sir, what would you like?" the waitress asks.

"How's the salmon?" I say.

The waitress is way too skinny to trust with such an important question. Probably had a spoon of low-fat yogurt and three deep breaths for lunch. Nothing more. She can't even sound enthusiastic when I ask her about the linguini.

In L.A., all the waitresses are too skinny. You can ask them about a soliloquy in *Hamlet*. Or to recite dialogue from the final episode of *Friends*. But never ask an L.A. waitress about food. From all appearances, they've never had any.

Instead, send out the chef. Let him waddle to the table, belch a couple of times, then describe what he'll eat when his shift is over. I prefer my dining advice from someone who daydreams about gravy, just like I do.

"I'll have the cod," I finally say, and immediately crave a good burger.

It is loud here in this Pasadena restaurant. Louder than a hundred babies. Classic rock screams from the speakers. Rod Stewart is hollering about how Maggie May is starting to show her age. It's a nice setting for an important meal. Like having dinner on a tarmac behind a jet bound for Singapore.

"Maggie, I wish I'd never seen your face!" Rod Stewart screams.

"AY! AY! AY! AY! AY!" the baby wails.

"AY! AY! AY! AY! AY!" I answer.

"AY! AY! AY! AY AY!" he wails again while banging his fists on the table.

"More bread?" I ask him, handing him a dinner roll.

"Why not," the baby says.

To my right, he sits. The baby's bare feet are like plump August tomatoes. They are soft and smooth and appear never to have touched the Earth. It is as if we keep him in a moist terrarium under a warm and constant light.

At the other end of the parenting spectrum sits my older daughter—freshly 21, sisters with the sun.

She is home from college for the summer with that leaky new puppy and that boyfriend with the guitar. With her back, the house is full again. Her laugh could warm Canada and significant parts of North Dakota. When she smiles, which is often tonight, her freckled nose crinkles and this dark restaurant seems to brighten.

I point this fact out to her mother, someone who appreciates the value of good lighting.

"She has nice white teeth," her mother explains.

"The best."

"That orthodontist did a really nice job," she adds.

He's not the only one. Blackjack, baby.

WE ARE GATHERED HERE TODAY...

THE BRIDE IS WEARING a beautiful white gown. We all know what white represents. That's right: surrender.

"You must become a student of your wife, Andrew," the minister is saying. "Anticipate her wants and desires, before she even voices them herself."

Now they tell me? In fact, had someone mentioned this at my own wedding, it would've saved me a lot of agony. When it comes to marriage, I almost never study. I've still got homework due from 1984.

The minister continues. A car alarm goes off, interrupting his next bit of advice.

"Andrew, that's the Lord's way of saying 'Listen up,'" the minister says.

I have been to a lot of weddings, perhaps too many. After college, there was a flurry of them. Who knows why exactly? I'm pretty sure we were brainwashed by our mothers. But believe me, a lot of those brains needed washing.

Back then, the receptions were like the closing ceremonies of childhood. Too much beer. Too much cake. Almost every weekend, another college buddy fell. Till there were no more buddies. Saturday nights have been pretty quiet ever since.

Two decades later, it is our children who are beginning to tie the knot. J. P. and Nancy, the neighbors down the block, are marrying off their eldest daughter, the one with the lemonade hair. The one who was just 12. You mean she's finished grade school? What do you mean she's done with college?

But for one afternoon time seems to stop. By the ocean's edge we gather—handsome Californians in linen and cotton and splotchy summer tans. A backdrop of blue. You can hardly tell where the sky ends and the ocean takes over.

And then there's that sea air. The breath of angels, this air. Nice job, God. For a single guy, you sure throw a nice wedding.

"Do you, Summer, take Andrew to cherish and to hold, till death do you part?" the minister asks.

"I do," she says.

Of course, she does. Only in Julia Roberts movies do brides back out at moments like this. Because in real life, the crowd would kill you. Everyone got all dressed up for nothing?

None of that drama here. It's a near-perfect ceremony in someone's near-perfect yard. The bride's brother leads a hymn. The minister elicits some light laughter. I'm a big believer in short weddings and long marriages.

The couple exchanges the two rings. We all know what that symbolizes. Little handcuffs.

"Ladies and gentleman," the young minister says, "I now present to you Andrew and Summer."

I'll tell you this about marriage. I still get chills at moments like this. Because, day in and day out, our own union has been an unabashed orgy of love, passion, and emotional intimacy. Christmas we take off, but every other day my wife and I have all those things. Obviously, it can be physically exhausting. It's amazing we both don't weigh, like, 11 pounds.

"Look at all the food," the little girl gasps inside the nearby reception tent.

"Finally," I say.

"Please don't embarrass us," my lovely bride says.

She's seen me at buffets before. She knows the dangers. By virtue of a cold and tiny heart, I am able to fit more free food inside my body than almost any other man. My motion with a fork resembles a racquetball serve.

"Did you taste these shrimp?" I ask my wife.

"How can you eat so much?" she wonders, with breathless disbelief.

"One big bite at a time," I explain through a wad of beef kebab.

Later, she warns me off dessert.

"They're very rich," she says.

"Really?" I say.

"Yes," she says, "you may only want three."

Fortunately, I have a baby to chase around. He toddles from one table to another locking eyes with any eligible woman under the age of 110.

He may be the next Brando, this baby. He doesn't talk so much as grunt and stumble around with an unexplainable charisma. Every time I look up, he's tunneling under some lovely stranger's dress.

"Where's your dignity?" I ask him at one point.

"Left it in the car," he says.

From table to table, he goes. He shows up, smiles, then goes right for the prettiest face. He favors the older ones, age 10 and up.

"You can't let him go like that," my wife says.

"I'll catch him," the little girl offers.

"Try to keep him off the cake," I say.

I have been to a hundred weddings. Most of the marriages lasted, some didn't. But I'll say this: I never lose faith. I never stop believing that it's the front-end of the rainbow.

For a thousand years from now, there may be no more oil. No more *Survivor* episodes. Even Ralph Nader may be gone. But one thing won't have changed. Human beings will still have weddings. Of all the mammals, we are probably the most hopelessly romantic.

Today, the young teacher with the lemonade hair is marrying the handsome future cop. Think there's a future there?

I do.

LORD OF THE WINGS

IT'S A NICE SUNDAY, with the sort of angled winter light that reminds you of the mountains. I spread out the sports section on the dining table, where a less-savvy host would place a boring tablecloth. Pay attention, you could learn a lot here.

"Mom says she's not coming," the little girl announces.

"Where?"

"To your party," she says.

My wife has never forgiven me, really, for my lack of input in our wedding planning. Should the salad be Caesar or mixed greens? Should the wedding singer have brown eyes or blue? Twenty years later, she is still getting even in a million tiny ways, like a scorned wife in an Updike novel. Flinty and unforgiving, but still delicious beneath that expensive makeup.

"But you're invited," I tell my wife.

"I just don't want to come to your Super Bowl party," she says.

"It's in your honor," I say.

"Um...no."

I didn't even get a chance to ask her about the salad: mixed greens or Caesar. She's out the door with that new baby of hers, who by the way is soaking up a lot of the extra attention I used to receive. After all these years, I've lost her to another man. One who wears diapers and plays all day with his tongue.

"Where's Mommy going?" the little girl asks.

"Paris. Rome. Maybe Milan," I say.

"Will she be home for dinner?"

Like a lot of today's children, our kids are never quite sure where their next meal is coming from. Could be Domino's. Could be from the sushi joint. Often, it is directly from the kitchen of their dear Italian mother, who learned to make a nice red sauce when she was all of 3. At our house, there are many potential sources for good food. What they are pretty sure of, our kids, is that their father isn't one of them.

And this is Super Bowl Sunday, the greatest and longest feast of the year. We will serve much the same fare you'd get at a Halloween party: chili, hot dogs, lots and lots of chips. It's far too important a meal to leave to a dad. Several courses. Tight deadline. Dip, seven layers deep.

"OK, everybody's going to help," I warn them.

"Where's Mom?"

"She went out."

"Where?" asks the boy.

"To Paris," sighs the little girl.

"Hilton?"

"No, that other Paris," I say.

When you split up like this, even if just for a couple of hours, it's important to maintain some sense of routine. Allegedly, kids value routine. I grab a bag of chicken wings from the freezer and squint at the directions.

"This oven, is it convection or conventional?" I ask.

"I think it's both," says the boy.

"Wow, we have a nice oven," I say.

"Dad, we've had it for about a year," notes the little girl.

I mean, I knew about the new refrigerator. It has this feature where you can chill a bottle of wine in minutes. I've never used it. But it's nice to know it's there. This new refrigerator also spits out ice cubes at such an alarming rate of speed that they will occasionally shatter the drinking glass you're holding. That's handy in a refrigerator—killer ice that bolts from zero to 60 in 1.2 seconds. Believe me, you're never standing around waiting. It comes to you, this ice.

The new oven, meanwhile, has more buttons than a schoolmarm's blouse. One says "convection." Another, "roast." Squinting again, I look for one that says "spicy chicken wings from Costco." No luck.

"This isn't a very good oven," I say.

"What time is the Super Bowl?" asks the boy.

"What time is Mom coming home?" asks the little girl.

"Do we have, like, a can opener, you think?" I ask, banging through cabinets, the essence of cooking.

I'll spare you the nasty details, but I have the sort of Super Bowl that Janet Jackson had, except that I manage to keep myself covered. Minutes before kickoff, a few of my buddies start to show up, which might be the real reason my wife left me. She generally likes my friends, except that they occasionally remind her too much of me, the guy who didn't help enough with the wedding. Really, I think it all goes back to that.

"Should the bridesmaids wear jewelry?" she asked me once, nearly a quarter-century ago.

"You know what might look good on them?" I said.

"What?" she asked.

"Handcuffs."

"This isn't your fantasy," she explained.

"It's not?"

"No, it's our wedding."

Over time, guys learn the difference.

"HI, JUST CALLING TO APOLOGIZE . . ."

ANSWERING MACHINE: We can't get to the phone right now. Please leave a message and we'll get back to you. Beeeeeeep:

Hi, you there? Oh, good, you're not there. Listen, my wife wanted me to call and thank you . . . wait, no, actually she wanted me to call and apologize . . . yeah, that's it, apologize. Something about your party last night, which we really enjoyed by the way, the parts of it we remember. You guys had a party last night, right? That's why I'm calling, I guess. Hey, you there?

Anyway, just wanted to let you know we had a really great time at your holiday party. And we really hope the thing with the drapes works out OK. Honestly, I was just trying to get the fireplace going a little bit better, and at the time those drapes made a great bellows. Who could know the sparks would fly around your living room like that, up in the ceiling fan and then clear to the staircase? Man, your house is really drafty. And that Christmas tree was really dry. Maybe you should water that tree a little more, huh? Well, I guess it's too late now. You see the way that firefighter dragged the flaming tree out of the house? Wow. You guys really throw great parties.

My wife also wanted me to tell you that there's a giant stain on the carpet, just outside the kitchen. I guess she caught me moving a table on top of it—or something—as if it was my fault. First thing this morning, she confronted me about it. Let me tell you, before that first cup of coffee in the morning, she's like Liza Minnelli.

By the way, what was that rocket fuel you were serving last night? Someone said it was a cosmopolitan. I say it was some sort of heroin martini. You used equal parts uranium and vodka, right? That's my guess. They sure were good, though. Like little glasses of candy cane water. At one point, I spilled a little on my new loafer and your dog licked it clear through to my sock. Don't worry about the shoe. There's more imitation leather where that came from, believe me. I just hope the dog is OK. Beagles that age, one drink and they're out. Bad drunks, beagles.

Anyway, every time I would turn around, you were refilling my glass. I want to thank you for that. This morning, I found three of those little cocktail party quiches in my coat pocket that I took but never ate. My wife says that's why we never get invited anywhere, because we're always taking food and drinking maybe a little too much. By "we," of course, she means me. At this very moment, a giant cement truck is driving around my brain, doing wheelies. An hour ago, I barfed up Berlin. Thanks for the cosmos, dude. Need that recipe soonest.

So that's why I called, just to apologize for whatever it was I did and to thank you and Kate for everything. As I always say, you have a very nice set of friends, and they made us feel very welcome. Nice friends. Does that Daphne always kiss with her tongue out? I'd like to rent your friends. Of course, I wouldn't have to rent Bruce, since he's a mutual friend. God, he was having a good time. He should've been wearing a toga. My wife said that if he hugged her one more time, she was going to tell his wife. Like his wife would've cared. You have great friends. Very tolerant. Very welcoming.

And your friend Doug. Did you know he's thinking about running for governor? Seriously. Maybe it was just the wine talking, but he says he thinks California is headed off in the wrong direction. When I left, he was passing around a recall petition on a dirty cocktail napkin. In California, is a cocktail napkin a legal document? I guess in this state, anything is.

And your buddy Jeff. He's in TV, right? Is that why he talks so loud? Was there a camera there? Was his microphone broken? Of course, I guess we were all talking too loud. By that third hour, I remember standing on our tiptoes in the kitchen and screaming at each other about Howard Dean's domestic policy or Nicole Kidman's real hair color, I don't remember. Everybody was yelling, but it was happy yelling, you know. Like we were in a locker room after a big game. Seriously, I love Jeff. Can he really get us into the Playboy Mansion? Call me about that, OK?

Anyway, buddy, really sorry about those drapes. Could've been worse,

I guess. If I hadn't pulled over your aquarium at just the right moment, the fire could've spread to the carpet, and then we really would've had a bad situation, let me tell you. But I'm sorry about those drapes. You had a designer, right? The wife wanted me to ask.

And the aquarium fish. They were the real heroes, not me. Were those the fish you brought back from Fiji on your anniversary? Jeeesh, sorry about the fish. I hope the insurance covers the little guys. My last recollection is of that beautiful neon tetra flopping around your couch pillow.

Well, listen, thanks again for the party. We'd like to have you guys over very soon, but you know, with the baby and all it's a little hard to entertain. The little guy has pretty much nursed her dry and the older ones are driving us both crazy. Did I tell you I'm doing a lot of the ironing now? The place is a mess. I can't even find the toaster. But, seriously, have us over anytime. We love you guys. We love your house, especially after the remodel. If you need any help with the smoke damage . . .

Answering machine: Beeeeeeep.

LURE OF THE GRILL

HERE WE ARE, heading back to our favorite butcher shop. To Porterville, California, we go. The city that never sleeps.

"He was married to one of those women with no lips," says my buddy Irv, "so her lipstick always looked crooked."

Irv is weaving stories as we zigzag our way to Porterville, a little farm town 50 tall tales from Los Angeles. It's like being on the road with a 45-year-old Tom Sawyer. The speedometer reaches 70. Irv's mouth tops 85.

"I wonder where we could find some good obsidian," Irv says. "I'm always forgetting the obsidian." Like cavemen, we're out searching for food, headed up to the little butcher shop that sells steaks as big as catchers' mitts.

It's a hunting trip, really, with bloodlust and adventure and all the things we occasionally lack in our day-to-day suburban lives. In the back are two giant coolers to hold the kill.

"If we could only find some obsidian," Irv says.

Along the highway, there are oil rigs, hundreds of the darned things, sculpted of Bethlehem steel, bobbing up and down in the heat. The pterodactyls of this California prairie.

"Black gold," I say.

"Texas tea," says Irv.

We come here every year or two to stock up on the best beef we can find. Sometimes before Christmas. Sometimes preceding some summer holiday. We have lists in our pockets: rib eyes, tri-tips, a few slabs of pork.

"My old man, he loved pork," Irv says.

"Whose didn't?" I ask.

"Dads, they all have their own uniforms," Irv recalls. "My old man, it was work pants and plaid shirts. That's all he ever wore."

When our mission here is done, we'll take our prey home and throw it on the grill, the most important piece of furniture we own. The grill will hiss at us. The neighbors will smell the smoke and envy our hearty summer incense. Our smoke signals to God.

Until then, Irv will talk incessantly about summer things. Grills. Sprinkler heads. Women. He's worried about women, not specifically but in a general way. Their behavior sometimes baffles him.

"It's women I worry about," Irv says as we zoom northward. "Why do they want to be like us?"

"Nobody should be like us," I say.

"The other day, I wax and wax the car," Irv says. "Eventually, know what I see in the reflection?"

"What?" I ask.

"Me," he says. "For all that work, you ought to see someone a little better-looking."

Up Highway 65 we go, past the orchards and the strawberry fields. The thermometer on the car reads 104. It's not yet noon.

"Ever tell you about my neighbor Tony?" Irv asks.

"No."

"He was a cop," Irv says, "in a little town with no crime."

We have this day trip all planned. First, we'll stop for breakfast, at a place where the egg yolks are as bright as the orange juice, not the sickly pale hue you see in the city.

Then we'll run over to a bar called Antlers. Finally, we'll stop at J&R Meat Co., where we'll pack the coolers in time for the Fourth of July.

"Rib eyes," I'm telling the manager 2 hours later.

"How thick?" he asks.

He slices and seasons them right there in front of us. Lean, these rib eyes. Direct from the Harris Ranch up the road.

"How are your New York strips?" Irv asks him.

Four hours later, I am back in L.A., making dinner for those people I live with, who sometimes seem to exist on soft drinks and breakfast cereal.

I fix them the first great backyard feast of the summer, celebrating the recent solstice and all the other summer holidays still ahead.

I shuck the sweet corn on the porch. I lay out the rib eyes on a grill that's hot as hell and almost as crowded.

"I hope they're not too big," I say.

"They look perfect," says my wife, who has a good eye for sizes.

The steaks grill up quickly. Black on the outside. Pink like a valentine within. Their smoke cloaks and seasons me. Till late October, I will smell of beefsteak and sunscreen.

Hello, summer, my old friend,

I've come to grill with you again.

"Nice salad, Picasso," says the boy when we all sit down to eat.

"Thanks," I say.

Happy holidays.

Our week in Malibu

BEFORE THE SUMMER ENDS, we thought we should get the children outdoors at least once. Introduce them to the sun. Familiarize them with fresh air. "Hey, Dad, what's that?" one will probably ask. "Sweetie, that's a tree," I'll answer.

I fear for the pasty-skinned children of America, who now shun the outdoors at every opportunity, content to sit inside and play Tetris all day on their cell phones or e-mail each other with catty comments.

Not my kids.

"We're going where?" the older daughter asks.

"Malibu," I explain.

"Yuck, Malibu," one of them says.

What could there ever be to do in Malibu? First, it's hemmed in on one side by a remarkable—but pretty dull—ocean. The other side is mountains and boutiques.

"Did Dad say 'boutiques'?" someone asks. And we're off.

We're house-sitting in Malibu, for about a week, and to spend a mere week in Malibu is like being squeezed fondly on the elbow by Marilyn Monroe. It's really not enough. But you remember it forever.

The air is sweet with salt and sage, the temperature just so. Malibu is what you get when you combine rustic beauty with near-perfect weather. So what if they don't have sewers.

"They don't?" my wife says.

"Maybe next year," I say.

But Malibu offers plenty of other pleasures. There is never "nothing to do" here. You can wander the beaches or climb the canyons. Ogle the local populace.

"I don't think they're all that great," my wife says after a trip to the grocery store for milk and ogling.

I don't know which populace she is seeing, but to me they all look pretty great. There is, it seems, a "Malibu" look," a sort of Western Gatsby. Many of the men have wavy Michael Landon hair. Surfer hair, it appears thickened with dried seawater and various crustaceans, living and dead.

The women? They are almost equally as pretty. They are thin and supple as oak saplings. Many look like the young actress Kyra Sedgwick. Those are the grandmothers. It just goes up from there.

"I think that's Cindy Crawford," my daughter whispers one morning in the pet shop.

"No," I say.

"Look, the mole," she says.

When she turns around, I see the mole, the world's most famous living mole. She is in the pet store with a small entourage of kids, nannies, nutritionists, skin-care specialists, hairstylists, seamstresses, accountants, and astrologers. Ah, the rich. They're richer than you and me.

"I'm pretty sure it's her," my daughter says.

It has been a busy week for the pretty people up here at Camp Malibu. The other evening, at Britney Spears' baby shower, somebody shot a paparazzo with a pellet gun. No one can tell me when the season for paparazzi runs up here, but I hear there is a three-photographer limit.

Another night, we think we see Amanda Bynes standing in line to buy frozen yogurt. They are everywhere, these celebrities. Toothy as their Lincoln Navigators.

"I saw Jessica Simpson," I tell the kids.

"Where?"

"She was buying motor oil," I say.

"No!"

Or maybe not. Point is, beautiful people are almost an epidemic up here. But they're still no rival for the rugged surroundings. Unspoiled. Vaguely Paleolithic. The beaches are dishwater blond. The sea, Dodger blue.

"I could live here," my wife says.

"Gas is a little expensive," I point out.

"They don't even have a movie theater," complains the older daughter.

Sorry, kid; it caught fire. The beloved Ben & Jerry's too. I guess no place is perfect. One day, while running to the beach, the toddler tumbled and scraped a knee. Basically, he outran gravity is what happened.

"The gravity here isn't very good," I told him later.

"There's not even a Burger King," noted the little girl.

Sunday night, sedated by the easy lifestyle, we don't even turn on the television. We just sit around letting the Malibu sun seep from our skin, enjoying a rare moment of total family unity. I don't really recommend it.

The kids complain that there isn't all that much to do, so I explain that this is a family vacation, and being around the people you love the most should be satisfying enough.

"Not for me," says the boy.

"What's your point, Dad?" says the older daughter.

So I entertain them with stories of wacky relatives they've never met, like the distant uncle who claimed to have invented the bottom of the coffee cup. You know, the part that keeps the coffee in.

"Before that, coffee used to pour out all over," I explain.

"It did?"

"Then your Uncle Bob came along," I say.

Then one night—the most exciting night—a little mouse sprang from the shadows and scampered through the kitchen. It was a lovely mouse. A sexy, Malibu mouse.

I think she'd had some work.

THE WASHING MACHINE
ATE THE BRA

IN OUR LAST INSTALLMENT, the Halloween decorations were going up late and somebody's bra was missing. I was having second doubts that family life was really for me. You know, just the usual stuff.

Since then, we have found the bra and discovered that we are the only house on the block in which the dog cusses. Not sure yet where he picked it up. Kids, probably.

"Are you sure he cussed?" I ask.

"I heard him," the little girl says, "with my own eyes."

In our house, we hear with our eyes, we smell with our ears, we reason with our hearts. I'm not defending it. If your house is operating flawlessly, please let me know.

"I found the bra," my wife says.

"Thank God," I say and flip the sports page.

Turns out that the bra—a wispy thing, a breath of air—disintegrated in the washing machine. Imagine a flock of doves flying innocently into a car wash, and you'll have a pretty good idea of what happened to this bra.

Now the washing machine is making an awful scratching sound, like something angry became trapped in there.

"Pliers!" I say authoritatively.

"Somebody get your dad some pliers!" their mother hollers.

"Thanks," I tell her.

"You're welcome," she says sweetly.

Now, I know nothing about washing machines. In minutes, I have the thing apart. The door is off. There is nothing wrong with the door, but I take it off anyway. While working, I notice that my fingers still smell of the onions I chopped the other night.

"You know what you're doing, Dad?"

"Absolutely not," I say.

"You're sweating."

"Here, hold this flashlight," I say.

The dog is nearby, hoping to pick up a few new cuss words. I am determined not to play into his base expectations. At times like this, rolling around the floor on a belly full of dinner, a father is expected to curse with frustration. You know, just to keep the top of his head from blowing off. Not me.

"Fu . . . dge," I say.

"Did Dad just say 'fudge'?" someone asks.

"Oh spit," I say.

The culprit, I soon find, is the underwire of the bra, a tiny strip of metal wedged between the outside of the washing machine drum and its metal shell.

When you turn on the washer, there's this scraping sound, metal against metal. You know how sometimes you put off getting your disc brakes fixed and before you know it you're grooving the rotors and doing even more damage? That sound. Like metal against your cerebral cortex.

I have unbolted the drain pipe, and am now reaching in up to my elbow with the needle-nose pliers, grasping desperately for the underwire of a bra that was probably bought on credit. It's like trying to snag a tiny brook trout at just the right moment. I have it, then I don't. Then I do. Then I don't.

The phone rings. The TV blares. The cat scratches to go out.

The microwave beeps. A shower starts. Somebody can't find a sharp pencil.

There is a toddler in a Spider-Man costume sitting on my ankles, playing with my shoelaces, in a way that kind of tickles. The dog sniffs my ear, enjoying my salty, fatherly musk (soon to be a popular cologne). Desperate after 20 years of marriage, I consider nuzzling him back.

"Got it!" I hiss.

"You did?" says my wife.

"He did?" thinks the dog. "Who the #$%@& would've expected that?"

The whole place can breathe again, now that I have fixed the washing machine, our most precious appliance. Like most heroes, I am fussed over beyond reason, then quickly forgotten.

But I don't care. I have more projects in the works. Because, obviously, store-bought bras are lacking in craftsmanship. Today's bras are built the same way angels must be built, with compressed air and hope.

So from now on, I am making all the brassieres in our house by hand, on my workbench in the basement. You can do it too. A basic brassiere can be made with the tools found around the house, plus an acetylene torch and a blacksmith's anvil.

Supplies include:

- 1 bulletproof police vest
- 4 bags of Portland cement
- 8 rebar reinforcing rods
- 1 heavy-duty Master lock
- A car alarm

Note that these dad-built brassieres each weigh about 45 pounds and resemble an iron lung. But they are rugged, carry a lifetime guarantee and won't peel apart at inopportune times. Like at the prom.

The holidays will probably be our busy season. Please place your orders now.

TALK LIKE A MAN

HE ONLY KNOWS a couple of words—"Mom" and "cat"—yet his sentences seem to run on for days, starting on Tuesday and ending, say, on the following Thursday. He punctuates them with sighs and sneezes, foot-stomping and a form of toddler charades that reminds me of the way people run when their clothes are afire. The baby's favorite story, or at least the one he tells most often, is of falling off the chair and hurting his drinking hand. The story is like something Tolstoy might've penned, epic but at times endlessly indulgent. Not bad for a guy who knows only two words.

"Say 'Daddy,'" I prompt him.

"Cat," he says.

"Say 'Daddy,'" I try again.

"Cat."

"Good," I say. "Now say 'Cat.'"

"Cat," he says, then spins around proudly, like he just invented pride.

Verbally, he is all thumbs. His father, me, learned the language while growing up in Chicago and listening to the original Mayor Daley deny allegations of corruption on TV, using lots of "das" and "disses." The baby, in turn, learns the language from me. And you thought Latin was in trouble?

"Say 'dog,'" I say.

"Cat," he says.

"Perfect," I say.

His mother is concerned about his limited language skills, yet I remind her that some men lead long and successful lives by never talking more than the baby does right now. With some guys, all you can hope for is one or two words occasionally. Eventually, they grow up to be middle managers. And fathers-in-law.

"Some men are grossly uncommunicative," I tell her.

"You're kidding," she says.

"But sometimes that's good," I say.

The baby, of course, knows the word "Mom," and uses it liberally, stringing the word together like pearls, as in "Mom-mom-mom-mom-mom." He spouts it when she changes him, gently stripping him of his overalls with her soft, undertaker hands. "Mom-mom-mom-mom-mom," he yodels, her one-man cheering section, her Michigan Marching Band.

He will also shout it when she locks herself in the bathroom, seeking shelter and a moment's respite. The baby will stand outside the door and shout her name at decibels normally heard only at political rallies. He has no worries in the world, other than his mother being out of sight for more than a minute.

"Can you watch him awhile?" she asks after their 30th consecutive hour together.

"Sure," I say, grabbing him like a guitar.

"Say 'Dad.'"

"Cat," he says.

"Good," I say.

"Say 'Mom.'"

"Mom-mom-mom-mom-mom."

"You know, once would be enough," I say. "You only need to say her name once."

"Cat," he says.

"Gotcha."

The best is when the baby's teenage brother emerges from his bedroom. Talk about talkers. Having slept for 3 months and not eaten, he heads immediately for the cereal cupboard. He burps and pours a bowl roughly the size of St. Louis.

"What are you doing today?" I ask.

Grunt.

"Did you have fun last night?"

Grunt. Slurp.

"How's the cereal?"

Slurp. Grunt. Slurp.

Like Shakespeare, this kid. Shut up, will you, I can't get a word in edgewise. (Parents take note: For all the times teenagers test your sanity, there are moments like this that make it completely worthwhile. Slurp. Grunt. Slurp. Grunt. Burp.)

"Apparently, your big brother only knows two words," I tell the baby. "Maybe you could work with him a little."

"Cat," the baby says.

"No, not the cat," I say, "your brother. Your brother might benefit from hearing you speak."

"Mom-mom-mom-mom-mom."

He really only needs to say it once.

Moments later, the baby and the boy dig through boxes of musty Halloween costumes, looking for something that pushes the envelope, costume-wise, and attracts lots and lots of women.

"How's this?" the older boy asks.

"Cat," says the baby.

"Actually, it's a giraffe," the older boy explains.

The costume was once worn by the older boy, 100 years ago when he was this same age. He dresses his younger brother in the giraffe costume, then pronounces it perfect by high-fiving the little guy and throwing him squealing to the couch.

"What are you going to be?" I ask the teenager.

Grunt.

"Sounds great," I say.

And great it is. The older boy develops a costume from a blue shirt decorated with big wads of cotton. He fills a squirt gun and tests it on the kitchen sink.

"Who are you supposed to be?"

He pauses, like the answer should be obvious from the blue and white outfit and the squirt gun. I wait. He waits.

"I give up," I finally say.

"Partly cloudy, chance of rain," he grunts, then squirts the cat.

"Not bad," I say.

"I found it on the Internet," he says.

Count 'em, six words in a row, from the mouth of a teenager. Strung together like pearls.

EPILOGUE

SO, LISTEN, thanks for stopping by. Sorry the place wasn't in a little better shape. Oh lord, look at the walls. They probably have more fingerprints than an FBI lab. Sorry. Try to think of our smudges as folk art.

Hope the guest room was comfortable. We don't have a guest room? Oh, that's right. So how was the couch? A little lumpy?

Believe me, there are a lot of miles in that couch, a lot of memories—not to mention toy parts, hair clips, Tootsie Roll wrappers, and about $100 in pennies, nickels, and Chuck E. Cheese tokens.

You know, we don't let just anyone sleep on that couch. We cradled and cared for two infants on its cushions, waited past midnight for the teenagers to come home. We cheered World Series and Super Bowls, watched presidential inaugurations and popes pass on. Too often, we fell asleep on that couch, while trying to finish *ER* or reunion tours of Cream.

Yep, there's a lot of life in that old thing, maybe too much. If it were a car, it'd be a clunker. If it were an old mare, we'd reward it with a pasture deep in clover. But it's a couch. We're hoping to get one more year out of it, then send it off to the Museum of Metaphors. "The Circle-of-Life Couch," the display will say.

Anyway, thanks for coming . . . hey, hold on a second. Something just crawled onto my lap. He's 20 pounds of leprechaun, warm as a loaf of new bread. The toddler has found me. No good can come of this. He'll take your soul if you let him.

Oha[oshv[ovhodsoasovoih.

That was a little note from the toddler. He's a gifted writer. Young, insolent. He just signed a development deal with Sony to write screenplays. He'll be in second grade when the deal expires. We hope he has a future after that. But it's a tough town, Hollywood. Ask anybody. You can be over the hill at 6. Which explains so much of what passes for popular entertainment.

Drp[oadmf;ladspaopj adspodsapofajop.

These are the conditions I write under. A toddler squirming in my lap, burping milky burps, while a teenager scolds her mother in the next room, something about shoes. We have a lot of Cinderellas for one house. Two. Three. I lose count. For 10 minutes, they argue about shoes. There are screams, then gunfire. A screen door slams, followed by sirens. I swear, Pynchon never wrote under these conditions. Poor guy.

Waspsopa@#$%^&sio[appodi[papodopaid.

That's him again, the toddler. You can tell that he's still learning the language. He thinks that M's are W's and verbs are pronouns. I predict he'll someday edit one of the great American newspapers or maybe run a network, in which case it won't really matter whether he can spell or read. He's high energy and has the attention span of a raccoon. Those are noble traits these days, coveted by almost every corporation. He might even seek high office.

So, needless to say, you've just visited a pretty typical American house, where happiness is a new sweater, the dryer eats the socks, and the kids wake up more glorious each morning.

You won't ever find us in *Architectural Digest*, unless the magazine decides to do a big spread on "Homes Where You Have to Jiggle the Toilet Handle." Or "Homes With Cold Germs Big as Softballs." We'd be all over that issue.

Or how about "Homes Where Some of the Windows are Painted Shut," or even "Houses Where the Kids Play the Same DVDs Over and Over and Over Again"? We'd dominate an issue like that. We might even get the cover.

No, I'm afraid this house is nobody's masterpiece, nobody's idea of the American Dream.

Except maybe mine.

Thanks for coming by.